LEAD, FOLLOW
OR GET OUT OF THE WAY

INSPIRATIONAL STORIES AND QUOTES
ABOUT LEADERSHIP, COURAGE AND
THE REMARKABLE HUMAN SPIRIT

First Edition

Jonathan D. Rose, M.D., Ph.D.

Lead, Follow or Get Out of the Way

Inspirational Stories and Quotes About Leadership,
Courage and the Remarkable Human Spirit
First Edition

Publisher:
AuthorVista LLC™
P.O. Box 57, Pine, Colorado 80470
AuthorVista.com

© 2019 Jonathan D. Rose, M.D., Ph.D., CFE, CPP, PSP, PCI

International Standard Book Number:

ISBN-13: 978-0-578-22746-7 (Paperback)

The book's title is a derivative of a quote commonly attributed to
General George S. Patton, for which the publisher has not been able
to adequately verify. See page 91 for the original attribution. The cover
image and the use of intellectual property rights, including the "right
of publicity" as they pertain to General Patton and his likeness were
purchased from CMG Clearances, LLC, located at 10500 Crosspoint
Boulevard, Indianapolis, Indiana 46256.

Content layout and format by AuthorVista LLC™
Cover design by AuthorVista LLC™

DEDICATION

I have flourished because of the loving and unwavering support given me by my parents. Together, they instilled in me courage, gratitude, the desire to excel, and the ability to overcome all that challenged me. It is for this reason that I dedicate this work to them both.

*The most courageous have something
within them, a spirit which is bold, wise, and fearless.
The courageous possess righteous principles, but are not
fearless. For if you believe a person of true courage must
be found perfect, you might as well deny the sun
for it does not always shine.*

CONTENTS

ACKNOWLEDGMENTS

First, I thank the teachers, professors, and the many instructors who gave of themselves and taught me to read, write, and better understand the world around me. Without their virtues of devotion, patience, and wisdom, this work would have never been possible, no less imagined. I am forever grateful to them and those who similarly taught and endowed them.

I also thank my professional colleague and mentor, Eugene F. Ferraro. As I researched, puzzled, and wrote for that which seemed endlessly, Gene tirelessly encouraged and coached me.

And finally, I thank all those whose lives, stories, and wisdom contributed to the content of this book. Without them and their inspiring human spirit, the pages that follow would be empty, as would our hearts. God bless them, and may their lessons and insights never fail or abandon us.

PREFACE

While I have made every effort to properly credit, cite, and acknowledge those whose material or quotes I have used, in numerous instances it was impossible. Where it was possible, I noted the identity of the likely or most probable source. However, where that was not possible or unresolvable conflicts arose, I noted the source of the material as simply *anonymous*. To those whom credit is due, I humbly apologize. If those who know the proper source inform me of such, I will gladly make the correction in the next edition.

Material which is not credited, or identified as anonymous is mine. If by chance someone else was first to record those words, I again apologize. If informed of such, I will give credit where due in the next edition. My publisher's contact information can be found on the copyright page and in my afterword.

On a final note, the reader should know that this book was written so as to not require it be read cover to cover. It has been formatted so any reader, at any time, can merely open the book and begin to read and enjoy it. Useful are the true-life short stories which begin each chapter. You will also notice that I have added occasional endnotes to some of the stories. They are intended to provide additional details or insight not contained in the story itself.

So crack it open and dive in. I assure your enjoyment and promise your time will be well spent. Thank you and prepare to be *inspired*.

Jonathan D. Rose
Bloomfield Hills, Michigan

INTRODUCTION

Militaria has fascinated me for as long as I can remember. Though I was not one to "play army" or build "forts" with my young friends as a child, I found all things *military* captivating. As I grew older and advanced my studies in chemistry, engineering and medicine I found the time to obtain my private pilot's license. The experience was exhilarating. Like the famous pilots of wars and conflicts past, I too had become a real pilot! Bold, daring, and thirsting for adventure I imaged myself a combat aviator as I took to the sky. I eventually earned the coveted, multi-engine commercial license but chose not to become a commercial pilot…something I never regretted.

But as any pilot will tell you, commanding a multi-engine aircraft of any size, not only requires extensive training and skill, it requires no small quantity of courage. Not the kind of courage needed to confront an armed and dangerous enemy in war, but the kind of courage needed to confront one's inner most fears. Though, few things in life ever frightened me, flying nevertheless taught me to be unafraid. But as you read this book, you will not learn about me. Instead you will learn about some of the greatest Americans of modern times and the many great leaders that came before them. Warriors, many were, and heroes were so many. This book is about them—those who were capable of inspiring the timid, the weak, and the brave. These men and women changed our world and in doing so, they became icons. Aviation brought them into my life, I now bring them into yours.

So what of it and who should care? Well as it turns out their courage and that which they fostered in others, rests on the amalgamation of all of our most admired virtues—self-discipline, compassion, personal responsibility, perseverance, honesty, hope, and a thirst for victory. Consider personal responsibility. Some of us accept it, others don't. Although it is to their detriment, those who reject it consider the acceptance of personal responsibility as a choice, often made for mere convenience. They behave with little regard for that which they say or do, or the outcomes their actions produce. However there are others who cherish personal responsibility. Like the men and women found in this book, they innately recognize that every personal decision and its corresponding action has the potential to initiate a life-changing chain of events often of profound proportions. These individuals accept the notion that they are solely responsible for the decisions they make, even when they are faulty and the outcomes they produce are undesirable. They know how and when to accept responsibility. They recognize the importance of personal responsibility, and possess the humility to embrace it. Their reward is a fuller, more abundant life.

To our great fortune the world is filled with many such people. Though many of them are seemingly ordinary, they are all around us. They are wise, simple, and virtuous people. Their courage and wisdom is capable of profoundly changing our perception of virtuosity and all of the collateral obligations which adhere to it. In the pages that follow we will explore some of the timeless bits of wisdom they and others have offered us. We will see how their insights can influence our lives, warm our hearts, and when needed, soothe a badly bruised soul. And while you will recognize many of them by name, their contributions which personify the essence of goodness and courage, many names you will not know. Together, their experiences and observations serve as lessons in character and morality. Their stories should stimulate as well as inspire the humanity that resides in each of us—for they are heroes and *we* are their beneficiaries.

1 COURAGE

*Courage is not the absence of fear. It's not being completely
unafraid. Courage is having apprehension and hesitation.
Courage is living in spite of those things that scare us.
Courage is the faith that some things will change and others
never will. It is the belief that failure is not fatal,
but to carry on when it is almost certain.*

Murph was not the average youngster. At an early age,
he demonstrated an instinct to protect the fragile and
meek. To his friends Murph became known at the
Protector. Born on the 7th of May 1976 in Smithtown, New York
to Irish-American parents, he was immediately recognized for his
big heart and abundant courage. His father, Daniel Murphy was
a former assistant Suffolk County district attorney and a veteran
of the Vietnam War. No foreigner to serving one's country
himself, his father served as both an inspiration and role model
for the young *Protector*.

In eighth grade he stood up and protected a young boy with
special needs who was being pushed around and picked upon by
a group of older students. Murph intervened and physically

pulled the attackers away from the defenseless boy. It would be the only time the principal of the school had to notify Murph's parents of a disciplinary issue. To the principal's surprise, Murph's dad responded by thanking the principal for the recognition he had "given" his son and that he and his wife "couldn't be been more proud." Who knew that the scrappy eighth-grader would one day be thanked by his country and recognized by the President of the United States.

In 1994, Murph graduated from Patchogue-Medford High School and left home to attend Pennsylvania State University, or better known as Penn State. He graduated in 1998, with a double major degree in political science and psychology. Murph was engaged to be married to Heather Duggan with the ceremony scheduled for November 2005.

But to the surprise of few, on September 2000, he accepted an appointment to the U.S. Navy's Officer Candidate School in Pensacola, Florida. On December 13th of that year, he was commissioned as an Ensign in the U.S. Navy and began Basic Underwater Demolition/SEAL ("BUD/S") training in Coronado, California in January. Eleven months later he graduated with Class 236. Following graduation from BUD/S, he attended the United States Army Airborne School, SEAL Qualification Training and SEAL Delivery Vehicle (SDV) school. Murphy earned his SEAL Trident and checked on board SDV Team ONE ("SDVT-1") in Pearl Harbor, Hawaii in July 2002. In October 2002, he deployed with Foxtrot Platoon to Jordan as the liaison officer for Exercise *Early Victor*. Following his tour with SDVT-1, Murphy was assigned to Special Operations Command Central (SOCCENT) in Florida and deployed to Qatar in support of *Operation Iraqi Freedom*.

Murph was next assigned to SEAL Delivery Vehicle Team ONE as officer in charge of Alpha Platoon and deployed to Afghanistan in support of *Operation Enduring Freedom*. There Murph was the commander of a four-man reconnaissance team…their mission was to kill or capture a top Taliban leader, Ahmad Shah (code name Ben Sharmak), who commanded a group of insurgents known as the *Mountain Tigers*.

On June 28, 2005, just six months before his intended wedding, his team was dropped off by helicopter in a remote, mountainous area east of Asadabad in Kunar Province, near the Pakistan border. After an initially successful infiltration, local goat herders stumbled upon the SEALs' hiding place. Unable to verify any hostile intent from the herders, the team freed them. Hostile locals, possibly the goat herders they let pass, alerted nearby Taliban forces, who surrounded and attacked Murph and his small team. After Murph called for help, an MH-47 Chinook helicopter loaded with reinforcements was dispatched to rescue the team, but was shot down with an enemy rocket-propelled grenade, killing all 16 personnel aboard; eight SEALs and eight service members from the 160th SOAR search and rescue team.

As the ground battle with the Taliban fighters continued, SEALs Murph, Danny Dietz, and Matt Axelson were killed in the action. Marcus Luttrell was the only U.S. survivor and was eventually rescued, after several days of hiding while protected by the people of an Afghan village. All three of Murph's men were awarded the Navy's second-highest honor, the Navy Cross, for their part in the battle making theirs the most decorated Navy SEAL team in history.

Navy SEAL Team Leader, Lt. Michael Murphy was subsequently presented the Medal of Honor, awarded posthumously, during a ceremony at the White House on 22 October 2007. It reads:

For Conspicuous Gallantry

For conspicuous gallantry and intrepidity at the risk of his life and above and beyond the call of duty as the leader of a special reconnaissance element with Naval Special Warfare task unit Afghanistan on 27 and 28 June 2005.

While leading a mission to locate a high-level anti-coalition militia leader, Lieutenant Murphy demonstrated extraordinary heroism in the face of grave danger in the vicinity of Asadabad, Kunar Province, Afghanistan. On 28 June 2005, operating in an extremely rugged enemy-controlled area, Lieutenant Murphy's team was discovered by anti-coalition militia sympathizers, who revealed their position to Taliban fighters. As a result, between 30 and 40 enemy fighters besieged his four member team. Demonstrating exceptional resolve, Lieutenant Murphy valiantly led his men in engaging the large enemy force. The ensuing fierce firefight resulted in numerous enemy casualties, as well as the wounding of all four members of the team. Ignoring his own wounds and demonstrating exceptional composure, Lieutenant Murphy continued to lead and encourage his men.

When the primary communicator fell mortally wounded, Lieutenant Murphy repeatedly attempted to call for assistance for his beleaguered teammates. Realizing the impossibility of communicating in the extreme terrain, and in the face of almost certain death, he fought his way into open terrain to gain a better position to transmit a call. This deliberate, heroic act deprived him of cover, exposing him to direct enemy fire. Finally achieving contact with his headquarters, Lieutenant Murphy maintained his exposed position while he provided his location and requested immediate support for his team. In his final act of bravery, he continued to engage the enemy until he was mortally wounded, gallantly giving his life for his country and for the cause of freedom. By his selfless leadership, Lieutenant

Murphy reflected great credit upon himself and upheld the highest traditions of the United States Naval Service.

The U.S. Navy ship USS Michael Murphy, and several civilian and military buildings have been named in his honor. Lt. Murphy was buried with full military honors at Calverton National Cemetery on Long Island, New York not far from his childhood home. Unknown to many, Lt. Murphy's last name, is Irish Gaelic, meaning *sea warrior*, while in English we know them as our Navy's SEALs.

We become brave by doing brave things.
—*Aristotle*

One man with courage makes a majority.
—*President, Andrew Jackson*

Mistakes are always forgivable, if one has the
courage to admit them.
—*Bruce Lee*

Courage is not the absence of fear, but rather the
judgment that something else is more
important than fear.
—*Ambrose Redmoon*

It takes courage to grow up and become
who you really are.
—*E.E. Cummings*

It often requires more courage to dare to do right
than to fear to do wrong.
—*Abraham Lincoln*

Life shrinks or expands in proportion
to one's courage.
—*Anais Nin*

Courage is fear holding on a minute longer.
—*General George S. Patton*

I have been to the darkest corners of government
and what they fear is light.
—*Edward Snowden*

Nothing is impossible, the word itself
says 'I'm possible!'
—*Audrey Hepburn*

How few there are who have courage enough to
own their faults, or resolution
enough to mend them.
—*Benjamin Franklin*

Courage is contagious. When a brave man takes a
stand, the spines of others are often stiffened.
—*Billy Graham*

Courage is not living without fear. Courage is
being scared to death and doing the
right thing anyway.
—*Chae Richardson*

Courage is doing what you're afraid to do. There
can be no courage unless you're scared.
—*Eddie Rickenbacker*

The most courageous act is still to think
for yourself. Aloud.
—*Coco Chanel*

Faced with what is right, to leave it undone
shows a lack of courage.
—*Confucius*

We need the courage to face the truth about what
we are doing in the world and act responsibly
[enough] to change it.
—*Daniel Ellsberg*

Courage is not simply one of the virtues, but the
[essence] of every virtue at its testing point.
—*C.S. Lewis*

Be with a leader when he is right;
Stay with him when he is still right; But, leave
him when he is wrong.
—*Abraham Lincoln*

Your rights matter because you never know when
you're going to need them.
—*Lynn Davison*

Being a patriot doesn't mean prioritizing service
to government above all else. Being a patriot
means knowing when to protect your country,
knowing when to protect your Constitution and
knowing when to protect your countrymen.
—*Emily Wood*

It is curious that physical courage should
be so common in the world and
moral courage so rare.
—*Mark Twain*

The encouraging thing is that every time you
meet a situation, though you may think at the
time it is an impossibility and you go through the
tortures of the damned, once you have met it and
lived through it you find that forever after you
are freer than you ever were before.
—*First Lady Eleanor Roosevelt*

Perfect courage means doing unwitnessed what
he would be capable of with the
world looking on.
—*Francois de La Rouchefoucauld*

If you're not a target, you're a failure.
—*G. Gordon Liddy*

Creativity takes courage.
—*Henri Matisse*

Courage and perseverance have a magic talisman,
before which difficulties
and obstacles vanish into air.
—*President, John Adams*

A great leader's courage to fulfill his vision comes
from passion, not position.
—*John Maxwell*

Unless you have courage, a courage that keeps
you going, always going, no matter what happens,
there is no certainty of success.
It is really an endurance race.
—*Henry Ford*

If you're not acting on your beliefs then
they probably aren't real.
—*Alex Noble*

You can't kill ideas. But you can sure kill the
people who hold them.
—*G. Gordon Liddy*

Fall down seven times, get up eight.
—*Japanese Proverb*

There are no shortcuts to victory.
—*Japanese Proverb*

Truth is coming and it cannot be stopped.
—*Stark Able*

There is no living thing that is not afraid when it
faces danger. The true courage is in
facing danger when you are afraid.
—*L. Frank Baum*

When we are afraid we ought not to occupy
ourselves with endeavoring to prove that there is
no danger, but in strengthening ourselves to go
on in spite of the danger.
—*Mark Rutherford*

Courage doesn't always roar. Sometimes courage
is the little voice at the end of the day that says
'I'll try again tomorrow.'
—*Mary Anne Radmacher*

Courage is like a muscle. We strengthen
it with use.
—*Ruth Gordon*

Extraordinary people survive under the most
terrible circumstances and they become more
extraordinary because of it.
—*Robertson Davies*

Courage is the most important of all the virtues,
because without courage you can't practice any
other virtue consistently. You can practice
any virtue erratically, but [none]
consistently without courage.
—*Maya Angelou*

Courage is knowing that you're beaten
and forging ahead anyway.
—*Zach Wahls*

He who is not courageous enough to take risks
will accomplish nothing in life.
—*Muhammad Ali*

The brave man is not he who does not feel afraid,
but he who conquers that fear.
—*Nelson Mandela*

Above all, be the heroine of your
life, not the victim.
—*Nora Ephron*

Have the courage to follow your heart and
intuition. They somehow already know what you
truly want to become.
—*Abraham Lincoln*

Whatever you do, you need courage. Whatever
course you decide upon, there is always someone
to tell you that you are wrong. There are always
difficulties arising that tempt you to believe your
critics are right. To map out a course of action
and follow it to an end requires some of
the same courage a soldier needs.
—*Ralph Waldo Emerson*

Keep your fears to yourself, but share
your courage with others.
—*Robert Lewis Stevenson*

Often the test of courage is not to die but to live.
—*Vittorio Alfiere*

Courage is the discovery that you may not win,
and trying when you know you can lose.
—*Thomas Krause*

Nearly all men can stand adversity.
But if you want to test a man's character,
give him power.
—*Abraham Lincoln*

All our dreams can come true if we have the
courage to pursue them.
—*Walt Disney*

Sometimes you don't realize your own strength
until you come face to face with
your greatest weakness.
—*Susan Gale*

Courage is what it takes to stand up and speak;
courage is also what it takes to
sit down and listen.
—*Sir Winston Churchill*

Anything is possible, the impossible just
takes longer.
—*U.S. Marine Corps proverb*

Anonymously…

Courage is the display of grace
when under pressure.

Winning isn't everything, but
losing is nothing. True strength is keeping
everything together when everyone expects you
to fall apart.

Anyone can give up, it's the easiest thing in the
world to do, but to keep it together when
everyone else would understand if you
fell apart, that's true strength.

Courage involves the making of errors and
mistakes, for they are the necessary steps in the
learning process; once they have served their
purpose, those errors and mistakes should be
forgotten and not repeated.

A veteran - whether active duty, retired, national
guard or reserve - is someone who, at one
point in their life, wrote a blank check made
payable to "The United States of America," for an
amount of "up to and including my life."

It takes no courage to watch the suffering
of the weak and helpless.

And from the author…

Courageous is to think aloud when
no else is talking.

Courage is the art of restraining power and
authority, when doing so is unnecessary.
Courage isn't something most of us are born
with. It must be found, nurtured, and given the
opportunity to develop. Doing is the stimulant
and results are the reward.

They who hate only win when we hate
them back.

Claiming that you don't care about your privacy
because you have nothing to hide is no different
than saying you don't care about free speech
because you haven't anything to say.

We never know how strong we are until being
strong is our only choice.

It appears on occasion that moderation has been
called a virtue so as to limit the courage of others,
and console the undistinguished
and their lack of merit.

To hate the courageous is to hate oneself.
Courage is not limited to the battlefield or
fighting for that which is right. The real test of
courage is much quieter. It is doing right when
no one is looking, remaining faithful when alone,
enduring pain when there is no hope, and
standing tall in the face of your
enemy and his kind.

The courageous always seem to find the time to
check their fear at the door.

We must do the things we think we cannot; for to
do otherwise is the epitome of failure.
There is no sane being that is not afraid when
facing danger. The truly courageous face danger
even when afraid.

The courageous never see themselves as
courageous, they simply are.

Failure is only the opportunity to more
intelligently start over.

Hate and anger are man's most powerful
emotions; but they are only useful when
controlled and measured
with courage.

It takes more courage to suffer than surrender.
Regardless of the circumstance, you needn't think
there is nothing you can do;
You can always tell the truth.

The most reliable way to predict behavior,
is to control yourself and let others
do as they wish.

*"You will be courageous by doing courageous things," said the lioness to
her cub. To which the young cub replied, "I will not disappoint you for I
fear not the unknown but wish only the chance to demonstrate I am
brave." "Ah," said the lioness, "you need not demonstrate your bravery
to anyone—you must only reveal it to yourself."*

2 PERSEVERANCE

Few things can take the place of perseverance. Talent will not;
nothing is more common than unsuccessful people with talent.
Genius will not; the world is full of educated derelicts, nor
will beauty or brawn. Perseverance and its companion courage,
together determine our fate. Combined they are omnipotent
and when seized, they can change history.

Gaius Julius Caesar, known for his middle and last name (nomen and cognomen), *Julius Caesar* was a Roman politician, military general, and historian who played a critical role in the events that led to the demise of Roman Republic and the Rise of the Roman Empire.

Born 100 BC to a patrician family, the *gens Julia*, which claimed descent from Iulus, son of the legendary Trojan prince Aeneas, supposedly the son of the goddess Venus. The Julii were of Alban origin, mentioned as one of the leading Alban houses, which settled in Rome around the mid-7th century BC. The Julii also existed at an early period at Bovillae, evidenced by a very ancient inscription on what is assumed to have been an altar in that town, which speaks of their offering sacrifices according to the *lege Albana*, or Alban rites. The cognomen "Caesar" originated, according to Pliny the Elder, with an ancestor who was born by Caesarean section (from the Latin verb to cut, caedere, caes-).

In 60 BC, Caesar, Crassus and Pompey formed the First Triumvirate, a political alliance that dominated Roman politics for several years. Their attempts to amass power were opposed by the Optimates within the Roman Senate, among them Cato the Younger with the frequent support of Cicero. Caesar however rose to become one of the most powerful politicians in the Roman Republic through a number of his accomplishments, notably his victories in the Gallic Wars, completed by 51 BC. During this time, Caesar became the first Roman general to cross both the English Channel and the Rhine River, when he built a bridge across the Rhine and later crossed the Channel to invade Britain.

Caesar's wars extended Rome's territory to Britain and eventually all of Gaul. These achievements granted him unmatched military power and threatened to eclipse the standing of Pompey, who had realigned himself with the Senate after the death of Crassus in 53 BC. When the Gallic Wars concluded, the Senate ordered Caesar to step down from his military command and return to Rome. Leaving his command in Gaul meant losing his immunity from being charged as a criminal for waging unsanctioned wars. As a result, Caesar found himself with no other options but to cross the Rubicon with the 13th Legion, leaving his province and illegally entering Roman Italy under arms. This began Caesar's civil war, and his victory in the war put him in an unrivaled position of power and influence, thus becoming Rome's first dictator. In celebration he proclaimed himself "dictator for life", in Latin he was called the "dictator perpetuo" of all of Rome.

But the general in Caesar never left him. In honor of the enemies he defeated, he gave them citizenship to the Republic. He initiated land reform and support for veterans. He centralized the bureaucracy of the Republic and improved its efficiency and thus, the government's balance sheet. But what is largely forgotten is Caesar's leadership in battle and among his many virtues, was perseverance. It was that perseverance when combined with ingenuity, which made Caesar, the *Caesar* we know today.

In 52 BC. after six years of battling the tribes of Gaul who occupied what is now Belgium, Luxemburg and parts of the Netherlands, Switzerland, Germany on the west bank of the Rhine, and the Po Valley, in present Italy, Caesar came upon an army of 80,000 Gauls occupying the small but fortified village of Alésia.[1] Caesar immediately ordered his legions to build a siege wall encircling the entire village so as to confine his enemy and enable his annihilation of them. However, he quickly learned from his scouts that a force of more than 200,000 Gauls were on their way to crush him and his forces and free their Gauls that Caesar had surrounded.

Caesar's response was as daring as it was innovative. He ordered his legions to immediate build a second set of fortifications around the city. Thus, he had encircled Gauls in Alésia *and* encircled his forces with a second wall protecting them from the advancing Gauls outside it.

Military history records nothing else like it. Caesar had successfully surrounded an army larger than his and then found himself surrounded by yet an even large army. When the larger force of Gauls arrived and attacked, Caesar and his army found themselves outnumbered 6 to 1 and fighting the enemy in both directions. Impossible as is was, Caesar and his men won the battle. Leading his reserve forces out of the fortification onto the open battlefield, he defeated the army which had surrounded him, forcing the surrender of those which he had surrounded himself. The decisive victory brought peace to Gaul and soon, Caesar the emperor's throne.

A mere eight years later, on the Ides of March (15 March), 44 BC, Caesar was assassinated by a group of rebellious senators led by Gaius Cassius Longinus, Marcus Junius Brutus and Decimus Junius Brutus, who together stabbed him to death. A new series of civil wars broke out and the constitutional government of the Republic was never fully restored. Caesar's adopted heir Octavian, later known as Augustus, rose to sole power after defeating his opponents in yet another civil war. Octavian set about solidifying his power, ending the Roman Republic *and beginning* the era of what today, we know as the *Roman Empire*.

*Always fight your battles from inside your enemy
and allow him defeat himself.*

Success is a function of persistence and
doggedness and the willingness to work hard for
twenty-two minutes to make sense of
something that most people would
give up on after thirty seconds.
—*Alan Schoenfeld*

There are two ways of attaining an important end;
force and perseverance; the silent power of the
latter grows irresistible with time.
—*Anne Sophie Swetchine*

It's hard to beat the person that never gives up.
—*Babe Ruth*

Through perseverance many people win success
out of what seemed destined to be certain failure.
—*Benjamin Disraeli*

Remember, you only have to
succeed the last time.
—*Brian Tracy*

I think a hero is an ordinary individual who finds
the strength to persevere and endure in spite of
overwhelming obstacles.
—*Christopher Reeve*

Don't be afraid to give your best to what
seemingly are small jobs. Every time you conquer
one it makes you that much stronger.
If you do the little jobs well, the big ones will
tend to take care of themselves.
—*Dale Carnegie*

By gnawing through a dike,
even a rat may drown a nation.
—*Edmund Burke*

The practice of perseverance is the discipline
of the noblest virtues. To run well, we must run
to the end. It is not the fighting but the
conquering that gives a hero his title to renown.
—*Elias Lyman Magoon*

Failure after long perseverance is much
grander than never to have a striving
good enough to be called a failure.
—*George Eliot*

You go on. You set one foot in front of the
other, and if a thin voice cries out, somewhere
behind you, you pretend not to hear it,
and keep going.
—*Geraldine Brooks*

When you get into a tight place and everything
goes against you, till it seems as though you could
not hold on a minute longer, never give
up then, for that is just the place
and time that the tide will turn.
—*Harriet Beecher Stowe*

Perseverance is a great element of success. If you
only knock long enough and loud enough at the
gate, you are sure to wake up somebody.
—*Henry Wadsworth Longfellow*

The difference between perseverance and
obstinacy is that one often comes from a strong
will, and the other from a strong won't.
—*Henry Ward Beecher*

It is not enough to begin; continuance is
necessary. Mere enrollment will not make one a
scholar; the pupil must continue in the school
through the long course, until he masters every
branch. Success depends upon staying power.
The reason for failure in most cases
is lack of perseverance.
—*James Russell Miller*

You've got to say, 'I think that if I keep working
at this and want it badly enough I can have it.'
It's called perseverance.
—*Lee Iacocca*

I do not think that there is any other quality so
essential to success of any kind as
the quality of perseverance.
It overcomes almost everything,
even nature.
—*John D. Rockefeller*

Patience and perseverance have a magical effect
before which difficulties disappear
and obstacles vanish.
—*President, John Quincy Adams*

Life is not easy for any of us. But what of that?
We must have perseverance and above all
confidence in ourselves. We must believe that we
are gifted for something and that this
thing must be attained.
—*Marie Curie*

The drops of rain make a hole in the stone not by
violence but by oft falling.
—*Lucretius*

If you can't fly then run, if you can't run then
walk, if you can't walk then crawl, but whatever
you do you have to keep moving forward.
—*Martin Luther King, Jr.*

It always seems impossible until it's done.
—*Nelson Mandela*

It is a sin to be silent;
When it is your duty to protest.
—*Abraham Lincoln*

Determination and perseverance move the world;
thinking that others will do it for
you is a sure way to fail.
—*Marva Collins*

You may encounter many defeats, but you must
not be defeated. In fact, it may be necessary to
encounter defeats, so you can know who you are,
what you can rise from,
how you can still come out of it.
—*Maya Angelou*

I hated every minute of training, but I said,
'Don't quit. Suffer now and live the rest
of your life as a champion.'
—*Muhammad Ali*

What we do not see, what most of us never
suspect of existing, is the silent but irresistible
power which comes to the rescue of those who
fight on in the face of discouragement.
—*Napoleon Hill*

So long as there is breath in me, that long I will
persist. For now I know one of the

greatest principles on success; if I persist
long enough I will win.
—*Og Mandino*

There is genius in persistence. It conquers all
opposers. It gives confidence. It annihilates
obstacles. Everybody believes in a determined
man. People know that when he undertakes a
thing, the battle is half won, for his rule is to
accomplish whatever he sets out to do.
—*Orison Swett Marden*

Perseverance is more prevailing than violence;
and many things which cannot be overcome
when they are together, yield themselves up
when taken little by little.
—*Plutarch*

The brick walls are there for a reason. The brick
walls are not there to keep us out. The brick walls
are there to give us a chance to show how badly
we want something. Because the brick walls are
there to stop the people who don't want it badly
enough. They're there to stop the other people.
—*Randy Pausch*

Stubbornly persist, and you will find that the
limits of your stubbornness go well beyond the
stubbornness of your limits.
—*Robert Brault*

If I had to select one quality, one personal
characteristic that I regard as being most highly
correlated with success, whatever the field, I
would pick the trait of persistence.
—*Robert M. Devos*

Great works are performed not by strength,
but by perseverance.
—*Samuel Johnson*

Permanence, perseverance, and persistence in
spite of all obstacles, discouragements, and
impossibilities: It is this, that in all things
distinguishes the strong soul from the weak.
—*Thomas Carlyle*

Many of life's failures are people who did not
realize how close they were to
success when they gave up.
—*Thomas A. Edison*

With ordinary talent and extraordinary
perseverance, all things are attainable.
—*Thomas Foxwell Buxton*

The harder the conflict, the more glorious the
triumph. What we obtain too cheap, we esteem
too lightly; it is dearness only that gives
everything its value. I love the man that can

smile in trouble, that can gather strength from
distress and grow brave by reflection.
—*Thomas Paine*

I am not judged by the number of times I fail, but
by the number of times I succeed; and the
number of times I succeed is in direct proportion
to the number of times I fail and keep trying.
—*Tom Hopkins*

Perseverance is not a long race; it is many
short races one after the other.
—*Walter Elliot*

But the person who scored well on an SAT will
not necessarily be the best doctor or the best
lawyer or the best businessman. These tests do
not measure character, leadership,
creativity, perseverance.
—*William Julius Wilson*

Anonymously…

The greatest oak was once a little nut
that held its ground.

Remember that guy that gave up?
Neither does anyone else.

Many of the great achievements of the world
were accomplished by tired and discouraged men
who kept on working.

There is no telling how many miles you will have
to run while chasing a dream.

Defeat doesn't finish a man, only
quitting does.

It is hard to say which came first, the dream or
perseverance? No matter, dreams without
perseverance, are just dreams.

A man is not finished when he's defeated.
He's finished when he quits.

It is the responsibility of the expert to manage
the familiar and it that of the leader
to transcend it.

And from the author…

A hero is an ordinary person who finds the
strength to persevere in spite of the
opposition and the consequences of failure.

Saints are sinners who kept on trying.

Strength and perseverance are often confused.
Our struggles develop our strength, our courage
develops our perseverance.

The harder I toil the luckier I seem to get.
If one's attitude determines their altitude, then
perseverance determines the
speed of their ascent.

Determination is doing something others have
determined not to do.

The enemies you make by taking a stand
generally have more respect for you than a friend
you make by quitting.

Only I can destroy my determination,
others can only strengthen it.

Industry is the enemy of those who quit.

Strong souls are seared with scars.

Our perseverance is capable of
inspiring the uninspired.

A controlling mindset that may include meanness
of spirit and a frank demonstration of ego or an
outward display of conviction should
never be counted upon, for true perseverance
is demonstrated only by action.

Only if you have been in the deepest and darkest
valley can you ever know the magnificence it is to
be once more, on the highest mountain.

We cannot learn from one another while
shouting at each other until we speak soft enough
that our words can be heard as clearly
as our voices.

We have not the power to control events, only
the power of our will to overcome them.

I'd agree with you, if only you were right.

PERSEVERE

Drive the nail aright, boys,
Hit it on the head;
Strike with all your might, boys,
While the iron's red.

When you've work to do, boys,
Do it with a will ;
They who reach the top, boys,
First must climb the hill.

Standing at the foot, boys,
Gazing at the sky,
How can you get up, boys,
If you never try?

Though you stumble oft, boys,
Never be down-cast;
Try, and try again, boys,
You'll succeed at last.[2]

---

[1] Alésia exists today and remains a small town just an hour south of Paris by automobile.

[2] The poem was provided for inclusion in this book by Aiden Elliott as an expression of love and gratefulness for his beloved mother, Marjorie (Marge) Elliott and his grandfather, Dennis Elliott both of whom he credits his incessant perseverance. The poem seems to have first appeared in the book, *Beacon Third Reader* authored by James Hiram Fassett (1869-1930) and published in 1914 by Ginn and Company (New York). The full text of *Beacon Third Reader* can be found online at https://babel. hathitrust.org/cgi/pt?id=hvd.32044081498743& view=1up&seq=1 for which its copyright has expired.

3 FAITH

Faith is the complete trust or confidence in someone or
something. It is the belief in God, His power and His mercy.
It is the ability to believe when no one else believes.
Faith is the assurance of things hoped for and the conviction of
things yet seen or realized. It is neither oppressive
nor coercive, for it is an unshakable belief.
Thus, through life we walk by faith, not by sight.

Ned was born in Boston on Oct. 7, 1931. The son of a marine architect and navy officer, he was raised to respect his parents, treat others with kindness, and love God. He was handsome, athletic, and smart. He graduated from the U.S. Naval Academy in 1954 and arrived in Vietnam in September 1967 aboard the nuclear powered carrier, the USS ENTERPRISE.

The ENTERPRISE had arrived on Yankee Station on December 2, 1965, and at the time, the largest warship ever built. She brought with her not only an imposing physical presence, but also a lethal complement of warplanes and advanced technology. By the end of her first week in hostile waters, the ENTERPRISE had set a record of 165 combat sorties in a single day. By the end of her first combat cruise, her planes and aircrews had flown over 13,000 combat missions. But the record had not been achieved without cost.

On March 17, 1968, Ned and his Bombardier/Navigator, Dale Doss, launched in their A6-A Intruder on a night, low-level strike into the heart of North Vietnam. After their departure they emitted their first radio transmission indicating that they were "feet dry" and over land, proceeding stealthily to their target, a rail yard just north of Hanoi. It would prove to be their final communication.

Undated U.S. Navy photograph of Ned beside his A6 Intruder. Note the 500 pound M-82 bombs configured for low altitude/close-support bombing under the plane's belly and left wing.

The next day, Radio Hanoi announced the capture of Ned and his bombardier. Following what had begun as his 18th combat mission, suddenly he had become a prisoner of war.

Both Ned and Dale were transported to a filthy camp near the center of Hanoi, called by its prisoners, the *Hanoi Hilton*. There, Ned (like Dale and hundreds others), was beaten, tortured and held in solitary confinement. After 17 months he and Dale were reunited, and soon joined some of their fellow prisoners. For what seemed a lifetime, they sat, waited, and gave emotional support to one another. Then a miracle occurred.

Shortly before Christmas in 1970, Ned and 42 other American prisoners of war decided to break prison rules and hold a brief service in celebration of the birth of their savior. But their barbaric and inhumane guards stopped them. In their presence, Ned stepped forward and asked his emaciated fellow servicemen, "Are we really committed to having church Sunday? I want to know person by person." Fellow prisoner, Leo K. Thorsness, later recounted in a memoir, "When the 42nd man said yes, it was unanimous. At that instant, Ned knew he would end up in the torture cells."[3] The following Sunday, Ned stepped forward to lead a prayer session and was quickly hustled away by angry guards. The next four ranking officers did the same, one by one, they too, were taken away to be beaten. And then, Thorsness remembered, the sixth-ranking senior officer began, "Gentlemen, the Lord's Prayer—*Our Father*, who art in heaven, hallowed be thy name…And this time, we finished it." Realizing they were facing men who believed in a God they could only imagine, the humbled guards relented and no one was punished.

Lt. Commander Edwin A. Shuman III, known to his fellow comrades as Ned, remained incarcerated at the Hanoi Hilton for more than two additional years. But it was Ned, the downed navy pilot, a man of impeccable courage and unshakable faith, who had won the prisoners' privilege to collective prayer.[4]

It is better to believe than to disbelieve; in so doing, you bring
everything to the realm of possibility.
—*Albert Einstein*

It is only with the heart that one can see rightly;
what is essential is invisible to the eye.
—*Antoine de Saint-Exupery*

Faith is different from proof; the latter is human,
the former is a gift from God.
—*Blaise Pascal*

Faith obliterates time, annihilates distance, and
brings future things at once into possession.
—*Charles Spurgeon*

Just because you can't see it doesn't mean it isn't
there. You can't see the future,
yet you know it will come; you can't see the air,
yet you continue to breathe.
—*Claire London*

Faith is not simply a patience that passively
suffers until the storm has past. Rather, is a spirit
that bears things with blazing serene hope.
—*Corazon Aquino*

If we become completely whole-hearted we will
have love for all people and will seek in each

person what is most holy, what God has inspired
in him or her. And only then will there be no
danger of softening or twisting our witness. Why?
Because the capacity of our faith will no longer
be narrow. If we are not broad-hearted, we have
not yet grasped the meaning of faith.
—*Eberhard Arnold*

Only with faith in something even greater than
our own determination can we take the
final seemingly impossible steps
forward to lasting change.
—*Edward Grinnan*

Faith is walking face-first and
full-speed into the dark.
—*Elizabeth Gilbert*

Absolute faith corrupts as absolutely
as absolute power.
—*Eric Hoffer*

Only the person who has faith in himself is able
to be faithful to others.
—*Erich Fromm*

Faith is not merely hope, and it must be more
than belief; faith is a knowing of the heart.
—*Rev. Floyd and M. Elaine Flake*

If you have abandoned one faith, do not abandon
all faith. There is always an alternative to the faith
we lose. Or is it the same faith
under another mask?
—*Graham Greene*

Faith, like sight is nothing apart from God. You
might as well shut your eyes and look inside, and
see whether you have sight as to look inside to
discover whether you have faith.
—*Hannah Whitall Smith*

Back of every creation, supporting it like an arch, is
faith. Enthusiasm is nothing: it comes and goes.
But if one believes, then miracles occur.
—*Henry Miller*

Where faith is there is courage, there is fortitude,
there is steadfastness and strength...
Faith bestows that sublime courage that rises
superior to the troubles and disappointments of
life, that acknowledges no defeat except as a step
to victory; that is strong to endure, patient to wait,
and energetic to struggle...

Light up, then, the lamp of faith in your heart...
It will lead you safely through the mists of doubt
and the black darkness of despair; along the

narrow, thorny ways of sickness and sorrow, and
over the treacherous places of temptation
and uncertainty.
—*James Allen*

God has already done everything He's going to do.
The ball is now in your court. If you want success,
if you want wisdom, if you want to be prosperous
and healthy, you're going to have to do more
than meditate and believe; you must boldly
declare words of faith and victory over
yourself and your family.
—*Joel Osteen*

Out of suffering comes the serious mind; out of
salvation, the grateful heart; out of endurance,
fortitude; out of deliverance, faith.
—*John Ruskin*

Faith isn't the ability to believe long and far into
the misty future. It's simply taking God at His
word and taking the next step.
—*Joni Erickson Tada*

Faithless is he who says farewell
when the road darkens.
—J.R.R. Tolkien

We are twice armed if we fight with faith.
—*Plato*

Faith is a knowledge within the heart,
beyond the reach of proof.
—*Kahlil Gibran*

I claim to be an average man of less than average
ability. I have not the shadow of doubt that any
man or woman can achieve what I have, if he or
she would make the same effort and cultivate
the same hope and faith.
—*Mahatma Gandhi*

That's the thing about faith. If you don't have it
you can't understand it. And if you do,
no explanation is necessary.
—*Major Kira Nerys*

Don't pray for an easy life; pray to be
a stronger man.
—*John F. Kennedy*

Sometimes your only available
transportation is a leap of faith.
—*Margaret Shepard*

Your belief determines your action and
your action determines your results,
but first you have to believe.
—*Mark Victor Hansen*

Faith is taking the first step even when you
don't see the whole staircase.
—*Martin Luther King, Jr.*

Faith moves mountains, but you have to keep
pushing while you are praying.
—*Mason Cooley*

If patience is worth anything, it must endure to
the end of time. And a living faith will last in the
midst of the blackest storm.
—*Mohandas Gandhi*

The antidote to frustration is a calm faith, not in
your own cleverness, or in hard toil,
but in God's guidance.
—*Norman Vincent Peale*

Faith…when you come to the edge of all the light
you have, and are about to step off into the
darkness of the unknown, faith is knowing one of
two things will happen: There will be something
solid to stand on, or you will be
taught how to fly.
—*Patrick Overton*

Faith is the bird that feels the light when
the dawn is still dark.
—*Rabindranath Tagore*

Our faith comes in moments… yet there is a
depth in those brief moments which constrains
us to ascribe more reality to them than
to all other experiences.
—*Ralph Waldo Emerson*

Faith is the spark that ignites the impossible and
causes it to become possible. When a person's
faith is activated, it sets in motion supernatural
power that enables that person to do what he
normally would never be able to do!
—*Rick Renner*

Faith is to believe what you do not see; the
reward of this faith is to see what you believe.
—*Saint Augustine*

You can do very little with faith, but you
can do nothing without it.
—*Samuel Butler*

To believe only possibilities is not faith,
but merely philosophy.
—*Sir Thomas Browne*

Just as a small fire is extinguished by the storm
whereas a large fire is enhanced by it – likewise a
weak faith is weakened by predicament and

catastrophes whereas a strong faith is
strengthened by them.
—*Viktor Frankl*

Always attempt to do ten good-deeds per day. And
when approached by a person who says, "How
may I repay you?", Reply, "Go out and do ten
good-deeds". In doing so, good-deeds will
spread throughout the land.
—*Hindu Blessing*

Faith is daring the soul to go beyond
what the eyes see.
—*William Newton Clark*

Whether you think you can or think
you can't, you are right.
—*Henry Ford*

Henry Ford Without faith a man can do nothing;
with it all things are possible.
—*Sir William Osler*

Anonymously…

Faith is not just for the faithless.
Faith is not without worry or care, but faith is fear
that has said a prayer.

Every tomorrow has two handles. We can take
hold of it by the handle of anxiety,
or by the handle of faith.

Faith isn't faith until it's all you're holding onto.

Fortunately, faith is not squandered on
the faithless.

Faith is believing in something when common
sense tells you not to.

The finest jewel a man can have is a
commitment to himself. Should he
depart from this he loses his commitment,
ambition, drive, authority, and ultimately
his faith in himself.

Be patient with the faithful; sometimes
they're all you've got.

Faith makes things possible, not easy.

Character is a journey,
not a destination.

And from the author…

Faith is a wager, the bigger the bet, the
bigger the potential reward.

Tolerance implies no lack of commitment to one's
beliefs. Rather it condemns the oppression or
persecution intended by others.

Don't worry about the future, just go as far as you
can and let faith do the rest.

Sometimes faith isn't enough, but complete
faith almost always is.

Faith is about trusting God,
even when it seems God is not listening.

A man of courage is a man of faith.

If fear is cultivated it becomes stronger, if faith is
cultivated it becomes strength.

If you forfeit your faith and confidence in others,
unwittingly you will have forfeited
your faith in God.

Faith is passion without limits.

God looks after those who look after themselves.

It requires less courage to believe,
than that to be faithless.

A day helping only oneself, is a day wasted.

Without fail, the best lessons are not those which
teach us what to do, but those which teach
us what not to believe.

But what NOT to do; If you believe in God, God
will believe in you.

God never made a promise *you* couldn't keep.
Robin once shrieked, "Holy strawberries Batman,
we're in a jam now," to which Batman replied,
"Have faith Robin, this joke is on the Joker."

When fear knocked, faith answered. And lo,
no one was there.

The faithful are those who put themselves at
risk for the benefit of others.

Have faith in God and let the Marines do the rest.

Be careful what you pray for, you might just
receive it when you least expect it.

Give your enemies permission fail. But remember
that the faithful know that, sometimes
the dragon wins.

*Almighty and most merciful Father, we humbly beseech Thee, of Thy
great goodness, to restrain these immoderate rains with which
we have had to contend. Grant us fair weather for Battle.
Graciously hearken to us as soldiers who call upon Thee that, armed
with Thy power, we may advance from victory to victory,
and crush the oppression and wickedness of our enemies and establish
Thy justice among men and nations..*[5]

---

[3] Lt. Col. Thorsness, an Air Force pilot and recipient of the Medal of Honor
for heroics on a mission in April 1967, wrote what he had witnessed in his
memoir, *Surviving Hell: A POW's Journey* (2008), "I know I will never see a
better example of pure raw [faith] or ever pray with a better sense of the
meaning of the word."

[4] Lt. Cmd. Shuman was not without resentment. In a debriefing,
following his repatriation he told his military interviewers that if it were
not for the antiwar movement in the U.S. and celebrity sympathizers,
the treatment of the U.S. prisoners held by the North Vietnamese would
have been briefer and more civilized. He credited much of the

mistreatment and torture he and other prisoners suffered to those who sympathized with the enemy.

[5] Aptly named, *Patton's Prayer*, the prayer was written at the direction of General George Patton in the form of a request for better weather in order to more efficiently kill the Germans in the winter of 1944. The prayer was written by Chaplain James Hugh O'Neill. The Chaplain initial told Patton that it was not a customary practice to pray for clear weather in order to kill one's enemy. Patton's alleged response was direct, *"Chaplain, are you teaching me theology or are you the Chaplain of the Third Army? I want a prayer, Damn it!"* The prayer was ultimately printed and issued to each member of the Third Army comprised of approximately 250,000 American soldiers. Chaplin O'Neill died in 1972 and is buried in the Roselawn Cemetery, in Pueblo, Colorado.

4 FRIENDSHIP

A friend can be silent with us in a moment of despair
or confusion. A friend can stay beside us in our
greatest moment of fear and grief. A friend can tolerate
our defeat, loss, and humiliation on the battlefield. But only
the truest of friends are without envy and celebrate
with us our victories and triumphs.

J oan of Arc was a mere seventeen year-old peasant girl when she led a French Army to a momentous victory against the English at Orleans in 1428. Oddly, her place in history was product of a very odd but historic *friendship*. Born to Jacques d'Arc and Isabelle Romée, a peasant family in Domrémy in north-east France, Joan at the age of thirteen claimed to have received visions of the Archangel Michael, Saint Margaret, and Saint Catherine of Alexandria. She told everyone who would listen that voices were instructing her to support Charles VII, the Dauphin of France and assist him recover her country from English domination and oppression.[6]

At the age of 16, she asked a relative named Durand Lassois to take her to the nearby town of Vaucouleurs, where she petitioned the garrison commander, Robert de Baudricourt, for an armed escort to take her to the French Royal Court at Chinon. Baudricourt's dismissive and sarcastic response did not deter her. She returned a few months later in November and gained support from two of Baudricourt's officers: Jean de Metz and Bertrand de Poulengy. According to Jean de Metz, she told him that "I must be at the King's side…there will be no help (for the kingdom) if not from me. Although I would rather have remained spinning [wool] at my mother's side…yet must I go and must I do this thing, for my Lord wills that I do so."

Under the auspices of Metz and de Poulengy, she was given a second meeting, where she made a prediction about a military reversal at the Battle of Rouvray near Orléans several days before messengers arrived to report it. According to the Journal du Siége d'Orléans, which portrays Joan as a miraculous figure, Joan came to know of the battle through "grace divine" while tending her flocks in Lorraine and used this divine revelation to persuade Baudricort to take her to the Dauphin.

After arriving and having been received by the Dauphin's Court she begged for a private hearing with the handsome 26 year old Dauphin. So strong was her impression on the uncrowned King Charles VII during their private meeting authorized her to travel with his army to the siege of Orléans as part of a relief force. Without armor, battle equipment or supplies, she depended on donated items for her armor, horse, sword, banner, and other items utilized by her meager entourage. In the battle which ensued, she proved her courage and determination. She gained prominence and was renowned after the siege was lifted after only nine days.

Several additional swift and decisive victories led to Charles VII's coronation at Reims. At his coronation, he celebrated the young Joan of Arc and reminded all present she was his *friend* and that her courage in battle had saved their country.

The celebration was short-lived. On the 23rd of May 1430, her career as a leader ended with her capture by the Burgundians during a skirmish outside the town. Although this was otherwise a minor siege, both politically and militarily, the loss of France's most charismatic and successful commander was an important event of the Hundred Years' War. She was subsequently handed over to the English and put on trial by the pro-English bishop Pierre Cauchon on a variety of fictious charges. After Cauchon declared her guilty she was burned at the stake on May 20, 1431, dying at the age of nineteen.

In 1456, an inquisitorial court authorized by Pope Callixtus III examined the trial, debunked the charges against her, pronounced her innocent, and declared her a martyr. Years later in the 16th century she became a symbol of the Catholic League, and in 1803 she was declared a national symbol of France by proclamation by of Napoleon Bonaparte. She was beatified in 1909 and canonized in 1920. Joan of Arc is one of the nine secondary patron saints of France, along with Saint Denis, Saint Martin of Tours, Saint Louis, Saint Michael, Saint Rémi, Saint Petronilla, Saint Radegund and Saint Thérèse of Lisieux.

Joan of Arc has remained a popular figure in literature, painting, sculpture, and other cultural works since the time of her death, and many famous writers, playwrights, filmmakers, artists, and composers have created, and continue to create, cultural depictions of her for she shall ever be a *friend* and hero of France.

But in the end, among the many lessons she offered, the most insightful may well be:

"The freest of people don't necessarily have the best of everything; they just make the most of the opportunities that come their way."

The Dauphin of France

"We'll be friends forever, won't we, Pooh?" asked
Piglet. "Even longer," Pooh answered.
—*A. A. Milne,* Winnie-the-Pooh

The best way to destroy an enemy is to make
him a friend.
—*President, Abraham Lincoln*

Don't walk in front of me, I may not follow.
Don't walk behind me, I may not lead.
Just walk beside me and be my friend.
—*Albert Camus*

If you haven't learned the meaning of friendship,
you really haven't learned anything.
—*Muhammed Ali*

Do not save your loving speeches for your
friends 'til they are dead; do not write them on
their tombstones, speak them rather now instead.
—*Anna Commins*

The language of friendship is not words,
but meanings.
—*Henry David Thoreau*

A friend to all is a friend to none.
—*Aristotle*

The truth is, everyone is going to hurt you. You
just got to find the ones worth suffering for.
—*Bob Marley*

No man is a failure who has friends.
— *Clarence in a book inscription to George
from Frank Capra's* It's a Wonderful Life, *1946.*

True friendship is like sound health, the value of
it is seldom known until it be lost.
—*Charles Caleb Colton*

It is virtue, virtue, which both creates and
preserves friendship. On it depends harmony of
interest, permanence, fidelity.
—*Cicero*

False friends are like our shadow, keeping close
to us while we walk in the sunshine, but leaving
us the instant we cross into the shade.
—*Christian Nevell Bovee*

One measure of friendship consists not in the
number of things friends can discuss, but in the
number of things they need no longer mention.
—*Clifton Fadiman*

True friendship is like sound health.
The value of it is seldom known
until it be lost.
— *Charles Caleb Colton*

Friendship is unnecessary, like philosophy, like
art…It has no survival value; rather it is one of
those things which give value to survival.
—*C.S. Lewis*

There is nothing we like to see so much as the
gleam of pleasure in a person's eye when he feels
that we have sympathized with him, understood
him. At these moments, something fine and
spiritual passes between two friends. These are
the moments worth living.
—*Don Marquis*

Friendship with oneself is all-important, because
without it one cannot be friends with
anyone else in the world.
—*First Lady Eleanor Roosevelt*

The real test of friendship is can you literally do
nothing with the other person? Can you enjoy
those moments of life that are utterly simple?
—*Eugene Kennedy*

It is not a lack of love, but a lack of friendship
that makes unhappy marriages.
—*Friedrich Nietzsche*

A friend is someone who knows all about
you and still loves you.
—*Elbert Hubbard*

Be courteous to all, but intimate with few, and let
those few be well tried before you give
them your confidence.
—*President, George Washington*

A friend is someone who knows all about you
and still loves you.
— *Elbert Hubbard*

Never befriend an enemy.
— *General George S. Patton*

Be true to your work, your word,
and your friends.
—Henry David Thoreau

There is nothing I would not do for those who
are really my friends. I have no notion of loving
people by halves, it is not my nature.
—Jane Austen

Some come and leave, fulfilling a single purpose;
others, for a time or a season to teach us by
sharing their experiences; and last, a select few
who participate forever with relationships
that endure through eternity.
—Jaren L. Davis

Treat all friends as you do your paintings
—place them in the best light.
—Jennie Jerome Churchill

Friends are the family you choose.
—Jess C. Scott

Anybody can sympathize with the sufferings of a
friend, but it requires a very kind nature to
sympathize with a friends success.
—Oscar Wilde

Being honest may not always get you a lot of
friends, but it'll always get you the right ones.
—*John Lennon*

Friendship is always a sweet responsibility,
never an opportunity.
—*Khalil Gibran*

I think if I've learned anything about friendship,
it's to hang in, stay connected, fight for them, and
let them fight for you. Don't walk away, don't be
distracted, don't be too busy or tired, don't take
them for granted. Friends are part of the glue that
holds life and faith together. Powerful stuff.
—*Jon Katz*

I always felt that the great high privilege, relief,
and comfort of friendship was that one
had to explain nothing.
—*Katherine Mansfield*

We all need friends with whom we can speak of
our deepest concerns, and who do not fear to
speak the truth in love to us.
—*Margaret Guenther*

It's the friends you can call up at
4 a.m. that matter.
—*Marlene Dietrich*

Sometimes being a friend means mastering the art of timing. There is a time for silence. A time to let go and allow people to hurl themselves into their own destiny. And a time to prepare to pick up the pieces when it's all over.
—*Octavia Butler*

There is a magnet in your heart that will attract true friends. That magnet is unselfishness, thinking of others first; when you learn to live for others, they will live for you.
—*Paramahansa Yogananda*

The glory of friendship is not the outstretched hand, not the kindly smile, nor the joy of companionship; it is the spiritual inspiration that comes to one when you discover that someone else believes in you and is willing to trust you with a friendship.
—*Ralph Waldo Emerson*

We cannot tell the precise moment when friendship is formed. As in filling a vessel drop by drop, there is at last a drop which makes it run over; so in a series of kindnesses there is at last one which makes the heart run over.
—*Ray Bradbury*

Don't be dismayed at goodbyes. A farewell is necessary before you can meet again. And

meeting again, after moments or
lifetimes is certain for those
who are friends.
—*Richard Bach*

The strongest marriage is between two who seek
the same God, the strongest friendship
between two who flee the same devil.
—*Robert Brault*

I value the friend who for me finds time on his
calendar, but I cherish the friend who for me
does not consult his calendar.
—*Robert Brault*

How does one keep from 'growing old inside'?
Surely only in community. The only way to make
friends with time is to stay friends with people…
Taking community seriously not only gives us the
companionship we need, it also relieves us of
the notion that we are indispensable.
—*Robert McAfee Brown*

Always set high value on spontaneous kindness.
He whose inclination prompts him to cultivate
your friendship of his own accord will love you
more than one whom you have been
at pains to attach to you.
—*Samuel Johnson*

But friendship is precious, not only in the shade,
but in the sunshine of life; and thanks to a
benevolent arrangement of things,
the greater part of life is sunshine.
—*President, Thomas Jefferson*

Friendship is always a sweet responsibility,;
never an opportunity.
—*Khalil Gibran*

A true friend embosoms freely, advises justly,
assists readily, adventures boldly, takes all
patiently, defends courageously, and continues
a friend unchangeably.
—*William Penn*

A friend is one that knows you as you are,
understands where you have been, accepts
what you have become, and still,
gently allows you to grow.
—*William Shakespeare*

Anonymously...

Friends are people with whom you
dare to be yourself and your soul can be
named with them.

A real friend never gets in your way unless you happen to be going down.

If I had a flower for every time I thought of you my friend...I could walk through this garden called Life forever.

Friends are people with whom you dare to be yourself. Your soul can be naked with them.

Friends encourage others to talk about themselves. They say little about others and rarely speak of their own success or pain. For the truest friends are patient listeners.

You can make more friends in two months by showing interest in others than you can in two years by trying to get other people interested in you.

Friendship isn't a big thing— it's a million little things.

Friendship is like a bank account. You cannot continue to draw upon it without making periodic deposits.

Before you accept the opinion of a friend or acquaintance who tells you that you are genius,

take a moment and reflect on what you thought
of their opinions in the past.

A good rule is not to talk about money with a
friend who has much more or
much less than you.

The reason dogs have so many friends is
because they wag their tails and
not their tongues.

Choose your friends by their character and your
socks by their color. Choosing your socks by
their character is vain, and choosing your friends
by their color is unthinkable.
A friend is someone who understands your past,
believes in your future, and accepts you
just the way you are.

True friends are those who care without
hesitation, remember without limitation, forgive
without any explanation, and love with
even little communication.

To each one of us friendship has a different
meaning. For all of us it is a gift. Friendship
needs to be cherished and nurtured. It needs to
be cultivated on a daily basis. Then shall it
germinate and yield its fruit.

Make friends with many and let the police
firefighters, EMS, and the Marines do the rest.

Don't cry because it's over, smile
because it happened.

The words that escape a friend's mouth are 'I'll
be there when you say you need me,' but the
words that are unheard from a true friend's
heart are, 'I'll be there…whether you
say you need me or not.'

Our efforts develop our strength, our
courage develops our perseverance, but it is
perseverance which ultimately triumphs
and so it is with friendship.

I came for friendship and left with love.

A friend of yours is a friend of mine.

And from the author…

True friendship brings with it true infinite duty.
The person electively formulating
the friendship owes a deep
and unquestioned loyalty.

A real friend is one who walks in at the very
moment everyone else walks out.

During the course of any human relationship be
it singular or collective, people will instinctively seek
out themselves. This may include influences from

physical features, educational history, religious
dispensation, or social groups.

It's funny they don't teach friendship in school, but
it is in school we find our first friends.

Friendships can sometimes be painful, but let's face
it, friends make life a lot more painless.

The best way to get a new friend is to be one.

Our best friends are happiest when we are, and
suffer the most when we are not.

Never laugh at the dreams of a friend.

Before you remind a friend of his faults, reflect
briefly on your own.

Friends will be friends.

A friend is someone who understands your past,
believes in your future and accepts
you just the way you are.

Envy is a waste of time and focus. But if you
must, focus on the needs of others and
waste time with a friend.

Being honest may not always get you a lot of
friends but it'll always find you
the best ones.

No friendship is tied with a bow, but every
friendship is a gift.

Be courteous to all, but intimate with few.

*All of us would like to have old friends. But old friends are not made in
a hurry. If you would like to have such friends in the years to come, you
had better start making new friends now. For our best friends are
like good wine, they get better with time.*

Joan of Arc

[6] Dauphin of France, originally Dauphin of Viennois, was the title given to the heir apparent to the throne of France from 1350 to 1791 and 1824 to 1830. The word dauphin is French for dolphin. At first the heirs were granted the County of Viennois to rule, but eventually only the title was granted.

5 HOPE

---

*Hope is the strength in your moment of weakness, the light in
the dark, the fire when it's cold. Hope is more powerful
than fear, and is the only antidote to despair. For when we
have hope, we can face even the most difficult challenges
in our path. Like courage, hope offers us the belief that
failure is not fatal, but the strength to carry on
when it is almost certain.*

The war was not going well. After having spent the
winter holed up in Cambridge, General George
Washington was anxious to drive the British from
Boston. His forces battered after their losses at Bunker Hill, were
eager to fight and expel the British once and for all. Washington
was no less anxious and was hoping for a decisive solution. That
solution was delivered to him by a 25-year-old bookseller-turned-
soldier, named Henry Knox.

Months earlier in November 1775, Washington had sent the
young Knox to bring to Boston the heavy artillery that had been
captured during battle at Fort Ticonderoga. In a technically
complex and demanding operation, Knox brought the valuable

cannons to Boston and delivered them to Washington in late January 1776. In March 1776, these artillery had been secretly positioned and now fortified Dorchester Heights (which overlooked Boston and its harbor), thereby threatening the British remaining one and only supply line, the sea.

Upon waking up on a frigid morning of March 17, 1776, the British commander, Sir William Howe saw the hills surrounding him brisling with cannon. At once he knew, Washington had thrown down the gauntlet and was prepared to destroy him and his army. Howe knew the British position at the foot of the hills surrounding him was indefensible and if he chose to fight, he and army faced certain destruction. What Howe did not know was that Washington's display of force was just that, a *display*. Washington's men and weapons were more than ready to destroy the British, but lacked enough gunpowder to fire a single shot!

Having concluded surrender was not an option, Howe ordered the withdrawal of all forces in Boston and hastily sent them to the British stronghold at Halifax, Nova Scotia. Following Washington's *siege*, the port-city of Boston effectively ceased to be a military target, but became a center of revolutionary activities, including the fitting ships of war and privateers. Many of its leading citizens would eventually play an important roles in the development of the future United States. To this day, Bostonians celebrate March 17th as *Evacuation Day*.

Learn from yesterday, live for today, hope for
tomorrow. The important thing is not
to stop questioning.
—*Albert Einstein*

The grand essentials of happiness are: something
to do, something to love,
and something to hope for.
—*Allan Chalmers*

Hope begins in the dark, the stubborn hope that
if you just show up and try to do the right thing,
the dawn will come. You wait and watch and
work: you don't give up.
—*Anne Lammott*

The very least you can do in your life is to figure
out what you hope for. And the most you can do
is live inside that hope. Not admire it from a
distance but live right in it, under its roof.
—*Barbara Kingsolver*

The feeling of hopefulness sometimes comes
from someone helping us. Think back to a time
when you had lost hope. Many times we regained
our optimism because someone
gave us a helping hand.
—*Catherine Pulsifer*

Never let go of hope. One day you will see that it
all has finally come together. What you have
always wished for has finally come to be. You will
look back and laugh at what has passed
and you will ask yourself…
'How did I get through all of that?'
—*Charles L. Allen*

Of all the forces that make for a better world,
none is so indispensable, none so powerful, as
hope. Without hope men are only half alive. With
hope they dream and think and work.
—*Charles Sawyer*

Most of the important things in the world have
been accomplished by people who have kept on
trying when there seemed to be no hope at all.
—*Dale Carnegie*

Hope is being able to see that there is light
despite all of the darkness.
—*Desmond Tutu*

Just as despair can come to one only from other
human beings, hope, too, can be given
to one only by other human beings.
—*Ellie Wiesel*

Where hope grows, miracles blossom.
—*Elna Rae*

Hope in a renewed future is one of the most
profound gifts of a life of faith.
—*David Hartman*

All kids need is a little help, a little hope, and
somebody who believes in them.
—*Earvin Johnson*

What oxygen is to the lungs, such is hope
to the meaning of life.
—*Emil Brunner*

Hope is the thing with feathers, that perches in
the soul, and sings the tune without the words,
and never stops at all.
—*Emily Dickinson*

Hope is both the earliest and the most
indispensable virtue inherent in the state of being
alive. If life is to be sustained, hope must
remain, even where confidence is
wounded, trust impaired.
—*Erik H. Erikson*

Hope never abandons you, you abandon it.
—*George Weinberg*

To love means loving the unlovable. To forgive
means pardoning the unpardonable. Faith means

believing the unbelievable. Hope means hoping
when everything seems hopeless.
—*Gilbert Keith Chesterson*

To be hopeful in bad times is based on the fact
that human history is not only of cruelty, but also
of compassion, sacrifice, courage, kindness. If we
see only the worst, it destroys our capacity to do
something. If we remember those times and
places where people have behaved magnificently,
this gives us the energy to act. And if we do act,
in however small a way, we don't have to wait for
some grand Utopian future. The future is an
infinite succession of presents, and to live now as
we think human beings should live,
in defiance of all that is bad around us,
is itself a marvelous victory.
—*Howard Zinn*

In all things it is better to hope than to despair.
—*Johann Wolfgang von Goethe*

None of us can continue to grow, develop and
perform at our highest potential without hope.
Hope for success, hope for recognition, and
reward, and most importantly, hope supplies the
essential fuel that enables the human spirit to
continue moving forward, especially in
the face of severe adversity.
—*John Di Frances*

We should not let our fears hold us back
from pursuing our hopes.
—*President, John Fitzgerald Kennedy*

A prime function of a leader is
to keep hope alive.
—*John William Gardner*

Hope is a beautiful thing. It gives us peace and
strength, and keeps us going when all seems lost.
Accepting what you cannot change doesn't mean
you have given up on hope. It just means you
have to focus your hope on more humanly
tangible and attainable goals.
—*Julie Donner Anderson*

We postpone the finality of heartbreak by
clinging to hope. Though this might be
acceptable during early or transitional stages of
grief, ultimately it is no way to live. We need both
hands free to embrace life and accept love, and
that's impossible if one hand has a
death grip on the past.
—*Kristin Armstrong*

There is a crack in everything, that's
how the light gets in.
—*Leonard Cohen*

If you lose hope, somehow you lose the vitality
that keeps life moving, you lose the courage to
be, that quality that helps you go on in spite of it
all. And so today, I still have a dream.
—*Martin Luther King, Jr.*

God puts rainbows in the clouds so that each of
us—in the dreariest and most dreaded moments
—can see a possibility of hope.
—*Maya Angelou*

Hope is always available to us. When we feel
defeated, we need only take a deep breath and
say, "Yes," and hope will reappear.
—*Monroe Forester*

There is no medicine like hope, no incentive
so great, and no tonic so powerful as
expectation of something tomorrow.
—*Orison Swett Marden*

The value of another's experience is to give us
hope, not to tell us how or whether to proceed.
—*Peter Block*

Hope is the ability to hear the music of
the future; faith is the courage
to dance to it today.
—*Peter Kuzmic*

Hope keeps you alive. Faith gives your life
meaning, blessings, and a good end.
—*Rex Rouis*

Hope is a powerful emotion that gives us
strength and helps us through trying and difficult
times. With hope, we believe that things will get
better, and we find the courage to keep trying.
—*Robert Alan Silverstein*

Where there is discord may we bring harmony.
Where there is error, may we bring truth.
Where there is doubt, may we bring faith.
Where there is despair, may we bring hope.
—*Saint Francis of Assisi*

The natural flights of the human mind are not
from pleasure to pleasure but from hope to hope.
—*Samuel Johnson*

Hope is the companion of power, and the mother
of success; for who so hopes strongly has
within him the gift of miracles.
—*Samuel Smiles*

Listen to the mustn'ts, child. Listen to the don'ts.
Listen to the shouldn'ts, the impossibles, the
won'ts. Listen to the never haves,

then listen close to me…Anything can happen,
child. Anything can be.
—*Shel Silverstein*

Hope is important because it can make the
present moment less difficult to bear. If we
believe that tomorrow will be better,

we can bear a hardship today.
—*Thich Nhat Hanh*

Man is, properly speaking, based upon hope, he
has no other possession but hope; this world of
his is emphatically the place of hope.
—*Thomas Carlyle*

Hope is not the conviction that something will
turn out well but the certainty that something
makes sense, regardless of how it turns out.
—*Vaclav Havel*

The word which God has written on the brow
of every man is Hope.
—*Victor Hugo*

Your hopes, dreams, and aspirations are
legitimate. They are trying to take you airborne,
above the clouds, above the storms,
if you only let them.
—*William James*

Anonymously…

They say a person needs only three things:
someone to love, something to do, and
something to hope for.

When the world says, "Give up," hope whispers,
"Try one more time."

Never deprive someone of hope—
it may be all they have.

Life has no obligation to give us what
we expect.

When the door of happiness closes, another
opens, but often times we look so long at the
closed door that we don't see the one which has
been opened for us.

It is possible that a single tomorrow
can make up for a whole lot
of yesterdays.

When things are bad, we take comfort in the
thought that they could always be worse.
And when they are, we find hope in

the thought that things are so bad they
have to get better.

He who has health, has hope. And he who has
hope, has everything.

And from the author…

Hope is a skill, without practice one
never seems to get good at it.

My hope is that courage trumps fear, my fear is
that those without hope are also without courage.
Those without hope are often helpless. Yet those
without help are never hopeless.

Were I granted a single wish, I hope I would
have the sense to make
it a good one.

Cracks are through which light enters us.

Hope is not a strategy, it's what's left for those
without a strategy.

It is often in the darkest of
skies we see light.

No one is so irreparable that they
cannot have hope.

Of all things, the sun is the most hopeful. It
never fails to rise, no matter how terrible
the day before.

It appears to me that the Hope Diamond is just a
diamond, but those who find such treasures
must have never lacked hope.

While there is infinite disappointment,
we must seek infinite hope.

Sometimes our dreams fall apart, so better things
can come together.

If you find yourself at the end of your
rope, tie a knot and hold on.

The existence of libraries
is proof there is hope, and the existence
of war is proof we need
more libraries.

It takes courage to have hope. Courage is necessary because in spite of all the hope we might muster, it seems, at times not enough. So isn't it mysterious that acts of courage provide us hope while it is hope that comforts the courageous?

---

[4] Though among the first of the colonies to fight the British and form a colonial army, Massachusetts did not ratify the Constitution and join the new Union until February 6, 1788.

6 Duty

---

*He who we call Soldier, is our Army. No army is better
than its weakest Soldier, its poorest leader, or its least
effective weapon. But of these, it is only the Soldier who is
also a citizen. Thus it seems obvious that the highest
obligation and privilege of citizenship is that of
bearing arms for one's country and being the
best Soldier he or she can be.*

"Duty, Honor, Country, those hollowed words reverently dictate what you ought to, what you can be, what you will be", said Douglas MacArthur. Young, Richard or *Dick* as he liked to be called, probably never knew General MacArthur had said those words, but likely latter learned of the General's intense determination to defeat his country's enemies.

Dick enlisted as an aviation cadet in the Army Air Corps on November 22, 1940, in Lubbock, Texas. He was commissioned as a second lieutenant eight months later in July 1941 and simultaneously received this pilot's wings. Little did he know that a mere nine months thereafter he'd find himself swinging under a parachute over enemy occupied territory.

As the last one out, he anxiously stood over the escape hatch in the belly of his fuel-starved B-25. Staring into the black abyss extending 9,000 feet below him, he took a deep breath he leapt head-first into the unknown. It was the night of April 18, 1942, and he and 79 other brave Americans had just flown one of the most audacious and dangerous missions of WWII. Dick and his fellow crew members were part of Doolittle's Raiders. Hours earlier his B-25 and the others like it that had companied him, had attacked mainland Japan. Now unsure of his exact location after seeking refuge over mainland China, his plane run had run out of fuel and would fly no more.

Doolittle's Raid began as an outlandish idea. With no base close enough from which to strike Japan and avenge its secret attack of Pearl Harbor, military strategists decided to launch 16 land-based B-25s from the aircraft carrier, USS Hornet. Lt. Col. Jimmy Doolittle was to lead the mission with Dick as his co-pilot. Dick had volunteered for the mission after seeing a base bulletin board notice stating only: "WANTED: VOLUNTEERS FOR DANGEROUS MISSION". The crews trained furiously day and night, not knowing anything more than that their mission was *DANGEROUS*. Once satisfactorily trained but unprepared for what was to come, the crews and their 16 bombers were loaded on the Hornet and quickly put to sea.

Still not knowing their mission or target or even their location, on the morning of April 18th, the ship's crew was notified that the enemy had spotted the Hornet and the strike force would launch some 200 miles further from its "target" than planned, *immediately*. Hastily, the crews manned their aircraft and launched in heavy seas. In just over four hours they reached their target, the Japanese capital of Tokyo. Amid heavy flak and anti-aircraft fire, the 16 bombers dropped their payload and headed to the safety of mainland China and prearranged landing fields.

As dusk arrived and darkness enveloped them, with their fuel nearly depleted as a result of having to launch further from their target than anticipated, Doolittle ordered those remaining in the flight to abandon their aircraft while they still could and bailout. Dick had never jumped out of a plane; he hadn't even had parachute training. As the last to leave the unpiloted, tumbling aircraft, he took one final look to ensure he was the last man aboard. With a final deep breathe he leapt and pulled his ripcord so hard he accidentally punched himself in the face, giving himself what he later recalled as a, "a real shiner".

To his surprise he safely landed in a tree and at first light started in the direction of his plane's final path to what he thought was *safety*. After a day of evading Japanese soldiers looking for survivors of the enemy aircraft that unnaturally and silently had "fallen from the sky", Dick surrendered to friendly Chinese soldiers who politely lead him to a small building. Inside, in a dark room lit by only a single candle, sat his pilot, Col. Doolittle.

After 10 harrowing days of Chinese assisted escape and evasion, with the Japanese in hot pursuit, Doolittle and his surviving crew members reached the safety of the Nationalist controlled city of Chunking. All those who had not been captured or killed were smuggled through Japanese lines by Chinese guerrillas and an American missionary *John Birch* and were repatriated. All told, fifteen of the sixteen bombers were lost (one successfully landed in Russia), three crew members were killed in action, eight pilots were captured, three were executed and one died in captivity. But their bold attack shook the Japanese and foretold of their humiliating and costly defeat.[7]

Lt. Col. Dick Cole retired from the U.S. military in 1966. Col. Cole was the last surviving participant of Doolittle's Raiders. He was the only survivor to live longer than Jimmy Doolittle, who died in 1993 at age 96. Colonel Richard Cole, United States Air Force, died peacefully April 9, 2019 at age 103.

We sleep safely at night because rough men stand
ready to visit violence on those who
would harm us.
—*Winston S. Churchill*

Out of every one hundred men, ten shouldn't
even be there, eighty are just targets, nine
are the real fighters, and we are lucky
to have them, for they make the battle. Ah, but
the one, one is a warrior, and he
will bring the others back
—*Heraclitus*

It is astonishing how little one feels
alone when brave.
—*John J. Gayer*

Success is how high you bounce when
you hit bottom.
— *General George S. Patton*

Darkness cannot drive out darkness: only light
can do that. Hate cannot drive out hate:
only courage can do that.
—*Martin Luther King, Jr.*

The day the soldiers stop bringing you their
problems is the day you stopped leading them.
They have either lost confidence that you can
help them or concluded that you do not care.
Either case is a failure of leadership..
—*General Colin Powell*

War is fighting and fighting means killing.
—*General Nathan Bedford Forrest*

Accept the challenges
so that you may feel the exhilaration of victory.
— *General George S. Patton*

It is fatal to enter a war without the will to win it
—*General Douglas MacArthur*

Love is that condition in which the happiness of
another person is essential to your own.
—*Robert A. Heinlein*

I would rather have eyes that cannot see; ears that
cannot hear; lips that cannot speak, than
a heart that cannot love.
—*Robert Tizon*

We accept the love (and compassion)
we think we deserve.
—*Stephen Chbosky*

A pint of sweat will save a gallon of blood
— *General George S. Patton*

You can depend so much on certain people, you
can set your watch by them. And that's (our
duty), even if it doesn't seem very exciting.
—*Sylvester Stallone*

If a man does his best, what else is there?
— *General George S. Patton*

Duty is the ability and willingness to allow those
that you care for to be what they choose for
themselves, without any insistence or assurance
that they will satisfy your expectations.
—*E.F. Ferraro*

Anonymously…

It takes only a minute to be heard, an hour to be
understood, and a day to respond—
but a lifetime to forget.

A sense of duty makes you a better person,
without changing you into someone
other than yourself.

The strongest actions for a soldier are to respect
herself, be herself, and shine amongst
those who never believed
she could.

It's true that we don't know what we've got until
we lose it, but it's also true that we don't
recognize a leader until
we meet one.

To the world you may be one person,
but to one person you may be their world.

Just because someone doesn't lead you the way
you want them to doesn't mean they are not a
leader, nor should it make you an
unworthy follower.

And from the author…

Wars may be fought with weapons
but they are won by men with a sense of duty.

It is the spirit of the men who follow
and of the man who lead
that determine victory.

It is our duty to never frown, even when sad,
because we never know who is watching us
and seeking our acceptance.

Duty often comes when we least expect it,
but seems to leave when we come to expect it.

A sense of purpose mends hate
and hate squanders our sense of duty.

You don't recognize your duty, it finds you—
often, where and when we
least expect it.

General George Smith Patton 1885-1945

We heard sheep, we drive cattle, we lead people;
Lead me, follow me, or get out of my way.[8,9]

.

---

[7] The John Birch society was established in Indianapolis, Indiana, on December 9, 1958, by a group of twelve led by Robert W. Welch, Jr., a retired candy manufacturer from Belmont, Massachusetts. Welch named the new organization after John Birch, the American Baptist missionary and military intelligence officer who was shot and killed by communist forces in China in August 1945, shortly after the conclusion of World War II. Welch claimed that Birch was an unknown but a dedicated anti-communist, and the first American casualty of the Cold War. Doolittle, who obviously met Birch and had spent time with him, following his Tokyo Raid, said in his autobiography that he was certain that Birch "would not have approved" of that particular use of his name.

[8] Reliably attributed to General George S. Patton. However, the quote has appeared in numerous forms in various works about the general and his war years.

[9] Unlike the image on the cover, the image on the prior page is in the public domain for which there are no known restrictions on publication or use. Most recently published in: the eBook *Great Photographs* by the Library of Congress, 2013.

7 DEDICATION

*No goal is achievable without overcoming
discouragement, obstacles and doubt. Achievers are resolute
in the pursuit of their goals and driven by dedication and
determination. But of these, only dedication can overcome the
darkness of defeat. So young soldier, yield not to those
who tug against you as you toil. Instead, let them perish
and savor forever, your victory over them.[10]*

I
n the summer of 1942 following the attack on Pearl
Harbor, like many young Americans eager to serve their
country, young Calvin decided it was time to enlist. With
head up, shoulders back he proudly walked into a recruiting
station in Fort Worth, Texas. Short in years but long in his
maturity, he had endured a difficult childhood. Born in the then
small town of Canton, Texas, his father had died young and his
mother had remarried. Calvin was unhappy but proud of his
heritage. After talking to an exuberant recruiter, he enlisted in the
U.S. Navy on August 15, 1942 and was shortly thereafter sent to
boot camp in San Diego, California, for six weeks. Upon
graduation he was immediately sent to Pearl Harbor at Oahu,

Hawaii, where he was assigned to the *USS South Dakota* in September.

It wasn't long before he found himself in harm's way. The *South Dakota* left Pearl Harbor on October 16. On October 26, 1942, he participated in the Battle of the Santa Cruz Islands. The South Dakota and her crew received a Navy Unit Commendation for the action. A month later on the night of November 14–15, 1942, Calvin was wounded during the *Naval Battle of Guadalcanal.* He had served as a loader for a 40 mm anti-aircraft gun and was hit by shrapnel while attempting to hand-deliver an important message to an officer in another area on the ship. Tossed down a stairway he was battered and bleeding from wounds he could not see. Though wounded himself, he bravely soldiered on and assisted his fellow sailors tend to the wounded and suffering. Through the night, he fought fires, carried the wounded to safety, and delivered messages to senior officers cutoff from their crew.

Severely damaged, the South Dakota left the Pacific and journeyed to the New York City naval yards on December 18, 1942, for an overhaul and battle damage repairs. She had taken 42 hits from at least 3 enemy ships and in order to make the Japanese think she had been sunk, the South Dakota was renamed "Battleship X". For his bravery and service during the battle, the young Calvin was awarded the Bronze Star and the Purple Heart, and like the others with whom he had served that night, he was awarded a second Navy Unit Commendation.

However, his navy career was about to come to quick and very disappointing end. Calvin's mother slipped and in a conversation revealed his age following her mother's funeral in Texas, during which he was in attendance. Not only had Calvin not received permission to take leave and go to Texas for the funeral, his

mother had revealed that *Calvin was only 12 years old!*
The bruhaha which resulted, landed Calvin in the brig where he sat for three months until his release following his sister's threat to contact the newspapers. Although he had tried to return to his ship, he was discharged from the navy on April 1, 1943 just two days before his 13th birthday. Sadly and inhumanly his awards were subsequently revoked. The South Dakota's gunnery officer, who was involved in the handling of what amounted to a court-martial, was none other than *Sargent Shriver.*

Shriver, like Calvin had volunteered and joined the US Navy. He spent five years on active duty, mostly in the South Pacific, serving aboard the *USS South Dakota*, reaching the rank of lieutenant (O-3). He was awarded a Purple Heart for wounds he received during the bombardment of Guadalcanal, just as the very young Calvin had.

Seaman Calvin Graham

Shriver later married Eunice Kennedy and in doing so became the brother-in-law of President John F. Kennedy. While subsequently serving in the Kennedy administration, Shriver founded and served as the first director of the Peace Corps from March 22, 1961 to February 28, 1966. And later after Kennedy's assassination, Shriver served as Special Assistant to President Lyndon Johnson. Shriver is best known as the *architect* of the Johnson administration's "War on Poverty".

Having never returned to school, Calvin joined the United States Marine Corps in 1948 at age 17. But once again his enlistment ended early when he fell from a pier and broke his back in 1951. Although serving in the Marine Corps qualified him as a veteran, he would spend the rest of his life fighting for full medical benefits and clearing his military service record.

In 1978, he was finally given an honorable discharge for his service in the Navy, and after writing to Congress and with the approval of President Jimmy Carter, all medals except his Purple Heart were reinstated. In 1988, he received disability benefits and back pay for his service in the Navy after President Ronald Reagan signed legislation that granted Calvin full disability benefits, increased his back pay to $4917 and allowed him $18,000 for past medical bills, contingent on him providing receipts for the medical services.

Calvin's Purple Heart was finally reinstated, and presented to his widow, Mary, on June 21, 1994, by Secretary of the Navy John Dalton in Arlington, Texas, nearly two years after his death from heart failure. The brave and very *dedicated*, Calvin Graham is buried at Laurel Land Memorial Park in Fort Worth, Texas.

I know why [we] were created with all [our]
imperfections. They humanize you. They are
made to make you forget yourself occasionally,
so that the beautiful balance
of life is not destroyed.
—*Anais Nin*

People's passion and dedication can
conquer anything.
—*Brie Bella*

Keep your dreams alive. Understand to
achieve anything requires faith and belief in
yourself, vision, hard work, determination,
and dedication. Remember all things are
possible for those who believe.
—*Gail Devers*

A man should never neglect his family
for business [or another woman].
—*Walt Disney*

What does it take to be a champion? Desire,
dedication, determination,
concentration and the will to win.
—*Patty Berg*

Success is about dedication. You may not be
where you want to be or do what you want to
do when you're on the journey. But you've got

to be willing to have vision and foresight
that leads you to an incredible end.
—*Usher*

We all have dreams. But in order to make
dreams come [true], it takes an awful lot of
determination, dedication,
self-discipline, and effort.
—*Jesse Owens*

I've always believed that success for anyone
is all about drive, dedication, and desire,
but for me, it's also been about
confidence and faith.
—*Stephen Curry*

I think most of my success is my dedication,
not my talent.
—*Anitta*

Confidence doesn't come out of nowhere.
It's a result of something... hours and days and
weeks and years of constant work
and dedication.
—*Roger Staubach*

The idea that [you can] push the envelope using
dedication and research and endless curiosity
has propelled [many a] life's work.
—*Randy Schekman*

Obstacles are those frightful things you see
when you take your eyes off your goal.
—*Henry Ford*

There is never just one thing that leads to
success for anyone. I feel it always a
combination of passion, dedication,
hard work, and being in the
right place at the right time.
—*Lauren Conrad*

There are no secrets to success. It is the result
of preparation, hard work,
and learning from failure.
—*Colin Powell*

Our truest life is when we are in dreams
while awake.
— *Henry David Thoreau*

Problems are opportunities dressed
in work cloths.
—*E.F. Ferraro*

The language of friendship is not words
but meaning.
— *Henry David Thoreau*

Anonymously…

Tomorrow is the only day of the year which
appeals to a lazy man.

My share of work may be limited, but
dedication to it is limitless.

When we dedicate ourselves to others,
it is impossible to be alone.

Think little goals and you can expect little
achievements.

It is hard to have interest in those
who have everything, yet offer nothing.

The most important things in life are your
friends, family, health, good humor, and
a positive attitude towards life.
If you have these then you
have everything!

While God is behind me, before me is eternity
and for that I am forever grateful.

And from the author…

Will is character and determination in action.

Without some form of dedication, a man alone in the world trembles in the cold.

Other things may change us, but we all start and end by ourselves.

Everyone needs a house to live in, but dedication to one's family is what builds a home.

If children learn to smile, hate, fear, enjoy life, love, laugh and cry from their parents, why haven't we more parents.

Great works are performed not by strength, but perseverance.

Determination expels extermination. If having a happy family were easy, everybody would have one.

The greatest waste is the difference between what we are and what we could become.

Live your beliefs and turn the
world around.

Dreams without actions are like
words without meanings.

Success is often found where its least expected.

---

[10] An adaptation from General George S. Patton by Jonathan Rose, Md. PhD.

8 WISDOM

---

*Wisdom is the ability to think and act using one's
knowledge, experience, insight, and intuition. It is not
inherited nor is it easily taught. It appears to be innate and
is expressed as a disposition to think and behave
with a willingness to consistently apply perception and
judgment with passion and reason. As such, it is the rarest
of all virtues—and arguably, the most allusive.*

Discretion is the better part of valor. A combination of
truth and wit, this ageless bit of wisdom was first
attributed to Falstaff in Shakespeare's *King Henry the
Fourth*, Part One. But while the combination of discretion and
valor is a rare commodity, in May of 1940 it was put on full
display.

The Miracle of Dunkirk is a tireless story of courage,
determination and strategy. The Dunkirk evacuation, code-
named *Operation Dynamo*, involved the evacuation of Allied
soldiers from the beaches and harbor of Dunkirk, in the north of
France, between May 26th and June 4, 1940. The operation
commenced after large numbers of Belgian, British, and French

troops were cut off and surrounded by German forces during the six-week long *Battle of France*. The disaster that followed was the by-product of Nazi Germany's invasion of Poland in September 1939.

Shortly after the German invasion of Poland, France and the British Empire declared war on Germany and imposed an economic blockade. In order to aid France, Germany's immediate neighbor to the west, the British Expeditionary Force (BEF) was sent to help the French. In response Germany invaded Belgium, the Netherlands, and then France on May 10, 1940. Three of its panzer corps attacked through the Ardennes and drove northwest to the English Channel. By the 21st of May German forces had trapped the BEF, the remains of the Belgian forces, and three French field armies along the northern coast of France. Commander of the BEF, General (Lord) Viscount Gort conferred with his peers and decided evacuation across the Channel as the best course of action and began planning a withdrawal to Dunkirk, the only suitable port for such a massive undertaking.

In addition to mobilizing its navy, British Admiralty issued a call for all sea worthy civilian boat and small craft owners to assist. A motley flotilla was quickly assembled and in spite of constant German aerial attack and bombardment, the civilian *"navy"* managed to rescue more than 338,000 men and deliver them to the safety of the English mainland.

Of the rescuers was a sixty-six year-old retiree. Charles was so determined to bring home as many evacuees he could, that he crammed 120 soldiers aboard his small motor yacht, the *Sundowner*. In spite the *Sundowner's* maximum safe capacity of 21 individuals, and the constant air threat, Charles delivered the men to safety and lost not a single soul. But perhaps his zeal to rescue others was driven in part by memories of a harrowing night in frigid waters of the North Atlantic nearly thirty years before. That night was April 14, 1912 and young Charles was the unfortunate Second Officer on the RMS *Titanic*. While he had assisted in the saving of dozens of lives that fateful night, Charles Lightoller was the last Titanic survivor to board the RMS *Carpathia*. Later in his testimony offered in the Christian Science Journal, he stated his faith in the divine power had provided him the ability to save himself and so many others. And again at Dunkirk, there appeared once more, divine intervention.

The Sundowner

But before the evacuation at Dunkirk had begun, on May 23rd a halt order was issued by the oberst General Gerd von Rundstedt, commander of Germany Army Group A. Adolf Hitler approved the order the next day and had the German High Command send confirmation to the front. Hitler decided that destruction of the trapped BEF, French, and Belgian armies ought to be left to the Luftwaffe. Realizing the mistake, the order was rescinded three days later, but it was too late. The failure to attack the trapped Allied forces ground troops provided the time they needed to construct defensive works and organize the evacuation.

A short while later on June 4th, lacking no shortage of wisdom Churchill offered his countrymen, "We must be very careful not to assign to this deliverance the attributes of a victory. *Wars are not won by evacuations.*"

Memory is the mother of all wisdom.
—*Aeschylus*

Good people are good because they've come
to wisdom through failure.
—*William Saroyan*

Wisdom is not a product of schooling but of the
lifelong attempt to acquire it.
—*Albert Einstein*

All human wisdom is summed up in two words—
wait and hope.
—*Alexandre Dumas*

Wisdom doesn't necessarily come with age.
Sometimes age just shows up all by itself.
—*President, Woodrow T. Wilson*

Knowing yourself is the beginning of all wisdom.
—*Aristotle*

By three methods we may learn wisdom: first by
reflection, which is noblest; second, by imitation,
which is easiest; and third by experience,
which is the bitterest.
—*Confucius*

Wisdom is like electricity. There is no permanently
wise man, but men capable of wisdom, who, being
put into certain company, or other favorable
conditions, become wise for a short time, as
glasses rubbed acquire electric
power for a while.
—*Ralph Waldo Emerson*

Wisdom is knowing what to do next, skill is
knowing how to do it, and virtue is doing it.
—*David Starr Jordan*

To everything there is a season, and a time
to every purpose under the heaven.
—*Ecclesiastes 3:1*

The wise man lets go of all results, whether good
or bad, and is focused on the action alone.
—*Bhagavad Gita*

The doorstep to the temple of wisdom is a
knowledge of our own ignorance.
—*Benjamin Franklin*

A wise woman wishes to be no one's enemy; a
wise woman refuses to be anyone's victim.
—*Maya Angelou*

A wise man proportions his beliefs
to the evidence.
—*David Hume*

The whole problem with the world is that fools
and fanatics are always so certain of themselves,
and wiser people so full of doubts.
—*Bertrand Russell*

Wisdom is the reward you get for a lifetime of
listening when you'd have preferred to talk.
—*Doug Larson*

A wise man can learn more from a foolish
question than a fool can learn from a wise answer.
—*Bruce Lee*

One must spend time in gathering knowledge
to give it out richly.
—*Edward C. Steadman*

Patience is the companion of wisdom.
—*Saint Augustine*

Wisdom is the right use of knowledge. To know is not to be wise. Many men know a great deal, and are all the greater fools for it. There is no fool so great a fool as a knowing fool. But to know how to use knowledge is to have wisdom.
—*Charles Spurgeon*

The wise person questions himself, the fool questions others.
—*Henri Arnold*

Wisdom is more precious than rubies.
—*Bible, Proverbs 3:15*

Wisdom is the power to see and the inclination to choose the best and highest goal, together with the surest means of attaining it.
—*J.I. Packer*

We are made wise not by the recollection of our past, but by the responsibility for our future.
—*George Bernard Shaw*

Knowledge speaks, but wisdom listens.
—*Jimi Hendrix*

Many men go fishing all of their lives without knowing that it is not fish they are after.
—*Henry David Thoreau*

We seem to gain wisdom more readily through our
failures than through our successes. We always
think of failure as the antithesis of success, but it
isn't. Success often lies just the
other side of failure.
—*Leo Buscaglia*

A single conversation across the table with a wise
man is worth a month's study of books.
—*Chinese Proverb*

Wisdom comes with the ability to be still. Just look
and just listen. No more is needed. Being still,
looking, and listening activates the non-conceptual
intelligence within you. Let stillness
direct your words and actions.
—*Eckhart Tolle*

Wisdom is not communicable. The wisdom which
a wise man tries to communicate always sounds
foolish... Knowledge can be communicated, but
not wisdom. One can find it, live it, do
wonders through it, but one cannot
communicate and teach it.
—*Hermann Hesse*

Wisdom is not wisdom when it is
derived from books alone.
—*Horace*

In seeking wisdom thou art wise; in imagining that
thou hast attained it—thou art a fool.
—*Lord Chesterfield*

It is unwise to be too sure of one's own wisdom. It
is healthy to be reminded that the strongest might
weaken and the wisest might err.
—*Mahatma Gandhi*

Wisdom outweighs any wealth.
—*Sophocles*

The young man knows the rules, but the old
man knows the exceptions.
—*Oliver Wendell Holmes, Sr.*

Never mistake knowledge for wisdom. One helps
you make a living; the other helps you make a life.
—*Sandra Carey*

To acquire knowledge, one must study, but to
acquire wisdom, one must observe.
—*Marilyn vos Savant*

Though wisdom cannot be gotten with gold,
still less can be gotten without it.
—*Samuel Butler*

There is no man...however wise, who has not at
some period of his youth said things, or lived a life,
the memory of which is so unpleasant to him that
he would gladly expunge it. And yet he ought not
entirely regret it, because he cannot be certain that
he has indeed become a wise man—so far as it is
possible for any of us to be wise—unless he has
passed through all the fatuous or unwholesome
incarnations by which that ultimate
stage must be preceded.
—*Marcel Proust*

Knowledge is proud that she knows so much;
Wisdom is humble that she knows no more.
—*William Cowper*

Mothers, teach your children this. Teach your
children that wisdom is everywhere. In pieces.
Some of the wisdom is in the trees, some of the
wisdom is with the animals. Some of the wisdom is
with the planets and the stars and the moons and
the sun. Some of the wisdom was with our
ancestors. Some of the wisdom is in our minds. All
of the wisdom is from the Spirit of God.
—*Esther Davis-Thomas*

Common sense in an uncommon degree is what
the world calls wisdom.
—*Samuel Taylor Coleridge*

Wisdom does not show itself so much in precept
as in life – in firmness of mind and a mastery of
appetite. It teaches us to do as well as to talk; and
to make our words and actions all of a color.
—*Seneca*

The art of being wise is the art of
knowing what to overlook.
—*William James*

True wisdom comes to each of us when we realize
how little we understand about life, ourselves,
and the world around us.
—*Socrates*

The first step in the acquisition of wisdom is
silence, the second listening, the third memory, the
fourth practice, the fifth teaching others.
—*Solomon Ibn Gabriol*

God grant me the serenity to accept the things I
cannot change, courage to change the things I can,
and the wisdom to know the difference.
—*The Serenity Prayer*

Great is wisdom; infinite is the value of wisdom. It
cannot be exaggerated; it is the highest
achievement of man.
—*Thomas Carlyle*

The wise know too well their weakness to assume
infallibility; and he who knows must know
best how little he knows.
—*President, Thomas Jefferson*

The writings of the wise are the only riches our
posterity cannot squander.
—*Walter Savage Landor*

Anonymously...

The wisest man is he who does not
believe he is wise.

Knowing others is intelligence; knowing yourself is
true wisdom. Mastering others is strength;
mastering yourself is true power.

No one can make you feel inferior without
your consent.

The way of a great man is three fold; virtuous,
he is free from anxieties; wise, he is free from
perplexities; and bold he is free from fear.[11]

It seems for some, what they lack in wisdom,
they offer in advice.

And from the author...

Not a tenth part of my wisdom is my own,
nor is it mine to keep.

It is through old things we learn
that which is new.

Wisdom without wit is worthless just as wit
without wisdom is useless.

Fear less, hope more, whine less, do more,
talk less, pray more, and good things will be yours.

Wisdom can either be earned or purchased. Those
who choose to purchase it, often
find it is easier earned.

Conventional wisdom is a myth. For if it existed,
wisdom would not be in such short supply.

We seem to think of failure as
the antithesis of success, but it isn't.
Success often lies just the other side of failure.

If results are a testament to our wisdom,
I wish I were wiser.

The truth is merely theory until proven otherwise.

The love of family and the admiration of friends
exceeds the value of wealth
and privilege.

Those without hope are often helpless,
yet those without help are
never hopeless.

*After his resignation from the Supreme Court, at the age of ninety-one,
Oliver Wendell Holmes, Jr. spent the summer at his country
house in Massachusetts. Several old friends from Boston came to visit,
bringing with them their grandchildren, whose company he immensely
enjoyed. Sitting on the porch one day, Holmes fell into conversation with
Betsy Warder, then sixteen. "I won't refrain from talking
about anything because you're too young," he remarked
with a smile, "if you won't because I'm too old."*

---

[11] An axiom similar to this one has been credited to Confucius. However, because of the many versions found, the author chose to cite it as *anonymous* and apologizes to Confucius.

9 HONESTY

Honesty is more than not lying. It is being sincere and
kind, thoughtful and thought-provoking. Honest people
don't hide their deeds and often share their
failures, for they know that to believe
in something and not to share it,
is dishonest.

What if you were an American hero and the very men whom you protected charged you with treason? Danny-Boy was born a natural explorer, woodsman, and frontiersman. During his long life of 86 years, his occupations included frontiersman, commercial hunter, trapper, soldier, teamster, state militia officer, politician, surveyor, merchant, sheriff, tavern keeper, horse trader, farmer and land speculator. However, he is most famous for his exploration and settlement of what is now Kentucky. In spite of violent resistance from American Indian tribes such as the Shawnee, he built forts, communities and blazed his *Wilderness Road* from North Carolina and Tennessee through Cumberland Gap in the Cumberland Mountains into what is today Kentucky.

In 1778 while leading a hunting party, he and several of the hunters were surrounded and captured by a heavily armed war party of Shawnee. Realizing his group was outnumbered, he convinced those who not yet captured to surrender without firing a single shot. According to later testimony, while in captivity Danny-Boy was overheard conspiring with his captors and British officers who had soon joined the Indians. They alleged the traitor, that in addition to a premature surrender to the Indians, Danny-Boy had attempted to negotiate the surrender of a nearby small town of which he was the founder. One of the former captives went so far as to claim the *traitor* took an oath of allegiance to the British!

Upon his release he was quickly placed under house arrest, charged with treason, and tried by court-martial. To the surprise of all present, Danny-Boy denied none of the facts. He stated however that his behavior was all part of a "stratagem" to deceive the British and save his town. He testified that after his capture he negotiated the surrender of the others in order to save their lives. He said he had in fact offered the surrender of the town so as to gain his release and warn those who lived in the town, a town of which had already been attacked once, during which he himself was the first man shot and wounded!

His testimony was most convincing. He was found not guilty of all charges. But hard feeling remained. Danial Boone left Boonesborough and returned to North Carolina to bring his family back to Kentucky. In the autumn of 1779, a large party of emigrants came with him, allegedly including the family of Abraham Lincoln's grandfather. Rather than remain in Boonesborough, Boone founded the nearby settlement of Boone's Station. He started a new business by locating good land for other settlers. The original Transylvania land claims had been invalidated after Virginia created Kentucky County, so settlers needed to file new land claims with in the new state of Virginia. The following year, Boone collected about $20,000 in cash from various settlers and traveled to Williamsburg to purchase their land warrants. While he was sleeping in a tavern during the trip, the cash was stolen from his room. Some of the settlers forgave Boone the loss; others insisted he repay the stolen money, which he in fact did.

Still recovering from financial difficulties, in April 1781, he was elected as a representative to the Virginia General Assembly, which was convened in Richmond. In 1782, he was elected sheriff of Fayette County. Captured again by the British near Charlottesville he was quickly released on parole. Boone returned to Kentucky and in August 1782 fought in the Battle of Blue Licks, in which his son Israel was killed. In November 1782, Boone took part in another Clark expedition into Ohio, the last major campaign of the war.

Bonne fathered 10 children. His youngest, Nathan Boone fought in the War of 1812, was a delegate to the Missouri constitutional convention in 1820, and a captain in the 1st United States Regiment of Dragoons at the time of its founding, eventually rising to the rank of lieutenant colonel. Three generations of Boone's descendants have been Major League Baseball players: Ray Boone, Ray's son Bob Boone, and Ray's grandchildren Bret Boone and Aaron Boone. The singer Pat Boone also claims to be a direct descendant. It remain unclear where Boone is buried. No less than three locations lay claim to his remains.

Anyone who doesn't take truth seriously in small matters cannot be trusted in large ones either.
—*Albert Einstein*

Honest hearts produce honest actions.
—*Brigham Young*

Honesty has a beautiful and refreshing simplicity about it. No ulterior motives. No hidden meanings. An absence of hypocrisy, duplicity, political games, and verbal superficiality. As honesty and real integrity characterize our lives, there will be no need to manipulate others.
—*Charles Swindoll*

And that's the thing about people who mean everything they say. They think everyone else does too.
—*Khaled Hosseini*

Slander cannot destroy the honest man – when the flood recedes the rock is there.
—*Chinese Proverb*

The real things haven't changed. It is best to be honest and truthful; to make the most of what we have; to be happy with simple pleasures; and have courage when things go wrong.
—*Laura Ingalls Wilder*

The first step toward greatness is to be honest,
says the proverb; but the proverb fails to state the
case strong enough. Honesty is not only "the first
step toward greatness,"—it is greatness itself.
—*Christian Nestell Bovee*

Almost any difficulty will move in the face of
honesty. When I am honest I never feel stupid.
And when I am honest I am automatically humble.
—*Hugh Prather*

All men profess honesty as long as they can.
To believe all men honest would be folly.
To believe none so is something worse.
—*President, John Quincy Adams*

Honest actions build a good reputation.
—*Donna B. Forrest*

The most exhausting thing in life
is being insincere.
—*Anne Lindbergh*

Honesty is the single most important factor having
a direct bearing on the final success of an
individual, corporation, or product.
—*Ed McMahon*

People grow through experience if they

meet life honestly and courageously.
This is how character is built.
—*First Lady Eleanor Roosevelt*

Liars when they tell the truth are not believed.
—*Aristotle*

Truth is like the sun. You can shut it out for a
time, but it's not going to go away.
—*Elvis Presley*

Truth is such a rare thing, it is a delight to tell it.
—*Emily Dickinson*

Don't bend; don't water it down; don't try to make
it logical; don't edit your own soul according to
fashion. Rather, follow your most
intense obsessions mercilessly.
—*Franz Kafka*

I hope I shall possess firmness and virtue enough
to maintain what I consider the most enviable of
all titles, the character of an honest man.
—*President, George Washington*

To make your children capable of honesty is the
beginning of education.
—*John Ruskin*

The best measure of a man's honesty isn't his
income tax return. It's the zero adjust
on his bathroom scale.
—*Arthur C. Clarke*

Honesty is the rarest wealth anyone can possess,
and yet all the honesty in the world ain't lawful
tender for a loaf of bread.
—*Josh Billings*

Honesty is the cornerstone of all success, without
which confidence and ability to perform
shall cease to exist.
—*Mary Kay Ash*

Do not do what you would undo if caught.
—*Leah Arendt*

I have found that being honest is the best
technique I can use. Right up front, tell people
what you're trying to accomplish and what you're
willing to sacrifice to accomplish it.
—*Lee Iacocca*

The easiest thing to be in the world is you. The
most difficult thing to be is what other people
want you to be. Don't let them put
you in that position.
—*Leo Buscaglia*

If it is not right do not do it; if it is
not true do not say it.
—*Marcus Aurelius*

Living with integrity means: Not settling for less
than what you know you deserve in relationships.
Asking for what you want and need from others.
Speaking your truth, even though it might
create conflict or tension. Behaving in ways that
are in harmony with your personal values.
Making choices based on what you believe,
and not what others believe.
—*Barbara De Angelis*

There are things to confess that enrich the world,
and things that need not be said.
—*Joni Mitchell*

A lie can travel half way around the world while
the truth is putting on its shoes.
—*Mark Twain*

We tell lies when we are afraid... afraid of what we
don't know, afraid of what others will think, afraid
of what will be found out about us.
But every time we tell a lie,
the thing that we fear grows stronger.
—*Tad Williams*

Life demands honesty, the ability to face,
admit, and express oneself.
—*Starhawk*

The only way you can truly control how you're
seen is by being honest all the time.
—*Tom Hanks*

Let's tell the truth to people. When people ask,
'How are you?' have the nerve sometimes to
answer truthfully. You must know, however, that
people will start avoiding you because, they, too,
have knees that pain them and heads that hurt and
they don't want to know about yours. But think of
it this way: If people avoid you, you will have more
time to meditate and do fine research on a cure
for whatever truly afflicts you.
—*Maya Angelou*

The first thing is to be honest with yourself. You
can never have an impact on society if you have
not changed yourself. Great peacemakers are all
people of integrity, of honesty, but humility.
—*Nelson Mandela*

If you do not tell the truth about yourself you
cannot tell it about other people.
—*Virginia Woolf*

It's discouraging how many people are shocked by
honesty and how few by deceit.
—*Noel Coward*

No legacy is so rich as honesty.
—*William Shakespeare*

Truth allows you to live with integrity. Everything
you do and say shows the world who you really
are. Let it be the truth.
—*Oprah Winfrey*

Never separate the life you lead from
the words you speak.
—*Paul Wellstone*

It takes two seconds to tell the truth and it costs
nothing. A lie takes time and [often]
costs everything.
—*Randi Rhodes*

Honesty is the first chapter in the book of wisdom.
—*Thomas Jefferson in a letter to Nathaniel Macon*

Honesty is a very expensive gift.
Do not expect it from cheap people.
—*Warren Buffet*

Truth is incontrovertible, malice may attack it and
ignorance may deride it, but, in the end, there it is.
—*Sir Winston Churchill*

A half-truth is a whole lie.
—*Yiddish Proverb*

Honesty and integrity are absolutely essential for
success in life—all areas of life. The really good
news is that anyone can develop
both honesty and integrity.
—*Zig Ziglar*

Anonymously…

If you want to ruin the truth—stretch it.

Honesty will be provided to the
extent it is demanded.

Look a man in the eye and say what you really
think, don't just smile at him and say what
you're supposed to think.

If you truly want honesty, don't ask questions you
don't really want the answer to.

The cruelest lies are often unspoken.

Inconvenient facts are often the most useful and
the most difficult to share.

The truth needs no rehearsal.

If it is not right don't do it; if it is not true,
don't say it.

Honesty is the first chapter in the book of wisdom.[12]

Sometimes the truth hurts but never worse than a lie.

And from the author…

Let's be honest, honesty is not always being
honest with others, most often it is
being honest with ourselves.

If we choose to play by our own rules and bend
the truth, we will eventually be governed
by the rules of others.

I've never met an honest man
who had no friends.

What is it that makes some men liars when the cost
of the words which comprise the truth
are so inexpensive?

The question, *what will happen if I tell the truth*, is an
admission disguised as a lie, and the answer, *if I did,
it was a mistake*, is a lie disguised as an admission.

Next to a faithful dog, honesty is often a
man's best friend.

Sadly, when someone prefaces a statement with, *to
be honest with you*, that which follows is often
neither honest nor sincere.

The true measure of one's success in life is not the
accumulation of wealth, but the number of friends
that believe us to be honest.

Honesty is having the belief in something
when common sense tells
us otherwise.

No matter where you go or what you do
you are always somewhere and
God is there waiting to
receive you.

---

[12] This quote is often attributed to Thomas Jefferson. However, numerous others have claimed it to be theirs. Thus the author cites it, anonymous.

10 DETERMINATION

Determination is an incredibly descriptive word. We use it to describe an unconditional commitment which has no limits or boundaries. Determination also describes a sense of purpose. For when we are determined, our world seems brighter, sharper, and more purposeful. We know without it, few things of Value would ever exist.

G race thought he was the most handsome man in the world. Tall, strong, and determined, he was all any young woman could have wanted. But all that remained of him, was a small engagement ring which bound two precious diamonds atop a small band of white gold.

Coming of age in Philadelphia in the late 40s was fun. It was a bustling city filled with adventure, opportunity, and *men*. The War had inspired great patriotism and many a teen, too young to serve, searched for a way to serve their country—Grace was no exception. As a teenager Grace dreamed of becoming a Navy nurse. Unfortunately, a reaction to a vaccination she received while in nursing school, ended her schooling and her dream. Severely disappointed, she began to worry about her future.

But her stretch of bad luck would end on a warm June day in 1950. On a blind date, Grace, met the love of her life. Bob was a seagoing Marine, with an enormous heart and sparkling eyes. After their first date, Grace was smitten as a kitten, and indeed, bitten by love. The months that followed were bliss. Soon talk of matrimony arose. Grace's heart was on fire. Then Bob popped the big question and asked for her hand in marriage. Their engagement was sealed with a gorgeous diamond ring. But suddenly, much to her astonishment, Bob disappeared! Without explanation or even a simple good bye, he had vanished.

"The heck with him," Grace thought. At the time she was 21. Living with her parents and in a job she hated, the 5-foot-8-inch firebrand, decided to take matters into her own hands and join the Marines. After overcoming a small medical obstacle, she was accepted. Ten days later she left a note for her parents, saying only—"Joined the Marines. Gone to Paris Island." After her swearing-in at the Liberty Bell, with orders in hand, she boarded a train and headed to boot camp.

Unlike many of the other women in her platoon, Grace did not find the training difficult, nor the discipline intimidating. Raised by a German father (a policeman no less), and a Scottish mother, her "childhood was worse," she later admitted. The physical training, marching, and spit-shined boots and shoes also came easy. On graduation day, she and over 80 other women in her company were promoted to *private* in the United States Marine Corps. In celebration they sang, *The March of the Women Marines*. It goes, in part…"We serve so men may fight in air, on land, and sea. Marines! The eagle, globe, and anchor carry on to make men free *for me*." The *"for me"* was, of course, tacked on for a laugh.

The young privates thought it was a gas.

Grace was like that, sharp witted, with an even sharper tongue. And in part because of it, she became a "plow-back." Such was the name given to those who stayed on at Paris Island as special instructors. These women were considered the best of the U.S. Marines. Not surprisingly, Grace knew it and showed it. Her performance was so impressive, Grace was later transferred to Washington D.C. to work for General Lemuel G. Shepherd, Jr., the Commandant of the Marine Corps.[13]

While there, Bob, the seagoing Marine who'd vanished several years before re-entered her life. She can no longer remember how they reunited, but the fire still burned in each of them. Several months later they were engaged again. The engagement did not last long. Several months after their engagement in October 1954, Bob called her one evening and broke it off. It wasn't another woman, he simply had cold feet. Heartbroken again, Grace trudged ahead in life without Bob.

In 1957 she left the Marine Corps and tried her hand at nursing school once more. And again she quit due to illness. "The work simply [made me sick]," she recalls. Then after a failed, twelve-year marriage, she re-entered school and this time graduated with degrees in sociology, psychology, and *nursing*. She eventually earned a master's degree and taught at Oklahoma Wesleyan University in Bartlesville.

Meanwhile, for 48 years Bob Meyers called another woman his wife. After her death in 2004, Bob once more thought of Grace and pondered the many years gone by. He was left with only a sad, "what-if?" But as luck would have it, while looking for a fellow Marine in an association directory, he found Grace. Fifty years and six weeks after he had broken off his second engagement with Grace, he called her the Sunday after Thanksgiving 2004.

The call lasted three and a half hours. They talked every night thereafter. During their call on New Year's Eve 2005, Bob proposed for a third time. Again Grace said yes! This time however, Grace Miltenberger-Meyers didn't need an engagement ring—she already had one. You see, Grace had kept the small diamond ring Bob first gave her more than 50 years prior. She had it taped to the bottom of a drawer for safe keeping, knowing one day she would need it. Bob and Grace married in November 2005 and have been happy ever since.[14]

Continuous, unflagging effort, persistence and
determination will win. Let not [them] be
discouraged who has these.

——*James Whitcomb Riley*

Never give up, for this is just the place and
time that the tide will turn.
——*Harriet Beecher Stowe*

Do not be too timid and squeamish about your
actions. All life is an experiment. The more
experiments you make the better.
—*Ralph Waldo Emerson*

I honestly think it is better to be a failure at
something you love than to be a
success at something
you hate.
—*George Burns*

When you blame others, you give
your power to change.
—*Douglas N. Adams*

Obstacles are those frightful things you see
when you take your eyes of
your goal.
—*Henry Ford*

Wishes are like seed…few ever develop
into something.
—*Michael Garofalo*

Let us not be content to wait and see
what will happen, but give us the
determination to make
right things happen.
—*Peter Marshall*

Procrastination is the theft of time.
—*Edward Young*

What you have to do and the way you have to do it
is incredibly simple. Whether you are willing
to do it, that's another matter.
—*Peter F. Drucker*

My God have mercy on my enemies,
because I won't.
—*General George S. Patton*

People do not lack strength, they lack will.
—*Victor Hugo*

You miss 100 percent of the shots
you never take.
—*Wayne Gretzky*

Tomorrow is the day when idlers work.
—*Edward Young*

The fight with dust.
—*General Erwin Rommel/Afrika Campaign*

Never tell people how do things. Tell them
what to do and they will surprise you.
—*General George S. Patton*

Anonymously…

The mind is all that matters.

Determination is and act, it is nothing
less than joy in action.

When the will is ready the feet are light

Small goals often yield the greatest
achievements.

Great will produces great power.

Age wrinkles the body, quitting
wrinkles the soul.

What may be done at any time, will
be done in no time.

And from the author…

For most, the belief *I can't* often means,
I won't. But few consider, the belief,
I can is the essence of *I will*.

Never fight if there is nothing to
gained by winning.

Every man should attempt to be
at the top of his field. That way, everywhere
he looks is down.

The world makes way for those
who have direction.

Will is character in action.

The real truth will never betray the man
who possesses it.

Guard your confidences carefully. Today's
friend may be tomorrow's
enemy.

Man's greatest waste is the difference between
what we are and that which
we could be.

Those who simply seek equality,
lack ambition.

---

[13] General Shepherd was the first Commandant to serve on the Joint Chiefs of Staff.

[14] With no small amount of celebration, Grace Miltenberger-Meyers was designated **Marine of the Year** by the Marine Corps League, Albert E. Schwab Detachment 857. VFW Post 577, 1109 E. 6th Street, Tulsa, OK 74120. See https://www.mclschwabdet857.com/index.html

11 Victory

We have nothing to offer but blood, toil, tears and sweat.
We have before us an ordeal of the most grievous kind.
We have before us hardship, suffering and disappointment.
It shall be our duty to wage war. We will serve and
sacrifice with all our might and with all the
strength that God may give us.
Our purpose is now victory and
may victory be ours.

G oing to war and serving one's country has never been easy. The pomp and circumstance, parades and farewells belie the horrors of things to come. Joe however, was nearly 34 years old and knew that which the future likely held. His eyesight had precluded his joining the Army, so instead he joined the Associated Press as a staff photographer but a short stint in Africa he decided he wanted to accomplish more. To his surprise the United States Maritime Service accepted him and soon served as a warrant officer documenting life at sea in enemy waters. In 1944 he rejoined the AP and followed the U.S. Army U.S. Marines into the Pacific Theater as a war correspondent.

But things got off on the wrong foot. While coming ashore his first day at Iwo Jima he slipped and fell overboard. Shook, but uninjured he pressed on. A few days later on the morning of February 23, 1944, he once again went ashore. Before arriving at the beachhead he heard a rumor that later that morning there was to be flag-raising atop an extinct volcano at southern tip of the island.

Upon landing, Joe hurried toward the base of the volcano. Wasting no time and lugging along his bulky Speed Graphic camera, the standard for press photographers at the time, he passed the dead and injured. Though the Marines had taken the island, the battle was not over. "The carnage was unthinkable", he later reported. Joining up with the exhausted Marine combat still photographer, Pvt. Bob Campbell and Marine color movie photographer Sgt. Bill Genaust, the small band began the climb up to the summit. About halfway up, they encountered Marine Staff Sgt. Louis Lowery, a photographer with the Marine publication *Leatherneck* on his way down after an enemy munition exploded on top and had knocked him off his feet and broke his camera. Lowery told them that the flag had already been raised at 10:40 a.m., and the only photos of the event where in his broken camera, which showed them.

Dissuaded but determined, the small group trudged on. Once atop the windy summit Joe discovered a group of Marines busy attaching a large flag to a length of steel pipe. Nearby, he saw the smaller flag which had been planted earlier, flapping away but barely visible. Under an officer's order, the smaller flag was hastily lowered with the idea of saving it for posterity. At the same instant Joe noticed the larger flag was nearly ready to be raised. As Joe was preparing his camera for the shot, six Marines grabbed the pole to which large flag had been attached and began to raise it. Without focusing his camera or looking into the viewfinder, Joe snapped away. Of the 11 images he captured, only frame 10 was worthy of reproduction. Bold and beautiful, the image the vision-impaired AP photographer, Joseph John Rosenthal had captured atop Mount Suribachi would soon capture the heart of every American. On Sunday, February 24, 1944 the photo appeared on the front page of every newspaper in the United States. Everyone who saw it, viewed it as a symbol of victory and American courage. Joe Rosenthal deservedly received the Pulitzer prize for his work and soon became the most famous war photographer in American history. Years later whenever asked about the photo, humbly responded, "I took the picture, the Marines took Iwo."[15]

What we do for ourselves dies with us. What we do
for others and the world remains
and is immortal.
—*Albert Pine*

You cannot expect victory and plan for defeat.
—*Joel Osteen*

No one has ever become poor by giving.
—*Anne Frank*

It is not what we get, but who we become, what
we contribute…that gives meaning to our lives.
—*Anthony Robbins*

The supreme art of war is to subdue the enemy
without fighting.
—*Sun Tzu*

Blessed are those who give without remembering.
And blessed are those who take
without forgetting.
—*Bernard Meltzer*

Step follows step, hope follows courage.
Set your face towards danger, and
set your heart on victory.
—*Gail Carson Levine*

No person was ever honored for what he received.
Honor has been the reward for what he gave.
—*President, Calvin Coolidge*

We should not let our fears;
Hold us back from pursuing our hopes.
—*President, John F. Kennedy*

Victory is to plant trees, under whose shade you
do not expect to ever sit.
—*Lord Nelson*

You have not lived until you have done something
for your country for which it can
never repay you.
—*General George S. Patton*

In all things it is better to hope
than to despair.
—*Johann Wolfgang von Goethe*

It is possible to give without loving, but it is
impossible to love without giving.
—*Richard Braunstein*

If there is any kindness I can show, or any good
thing I can do to any fellow being, let me do it
now, and not deter or neglect it,
as I shall not pass this way again.
—*William Penn*

The great use of life is to spend it for
something that outlasts it.
—*William James*

A half-truth is a whole lie.
—*Yiddish Proverb*

The best portion of a good man's life, his little,
nameless, unremembered acts
of kindness and love.
—*William Wordsworth*

Anonymously…

Be ashamed to die until you have won a victory
for mankind.

If you want to touch the past, touch a rock. If you
want to touch the present, touch a flower. If you
want to touch victory, touch a life.

I am only one. But still I am one. I cannot do
everything, but still I can do something. And

because I cannot do everything, I will not refuse to
do the something that I can do.

Dream what you want to dream; go where you
want to go; be what you want to be; because you
have only one life to live and one chance to do all
the things that need to be done.

The charitable give out the door and God puts it
back through the window.
Most of the important things in the world

have been accomplished by people who
sough victory of their oppressor.

The success of a people [is often]
ruined by their failure to acknowledge victory
is but a prayer away.

And from the author...

Take your victories, whatever they may be, cherish
them, remember them, and seek another.

Life is a battle...a true struggle.
Any person must find hope in himself;
and seek great duty to himself. In doing so he should
remember that victory over his opponent
is but one blow away.

Most of the important things in the world have
been accomplished by people who have
courage and sought victor.

When you are looking for obstacles, you won't
find victory.

As iron is eaten by rust, the envious are
taken by greed, the weak are consumed in battle.
There is no legacy richer than victory.

Give the enemy more than they expect
and do it cheerfully.

It may seem odd, but the more I fight,
the more victories I enjoy.

---

[15] Of the six Marines who raised the *second* flag, Frank Sousley, Harlan Block, and Michael Shank were subsequently killed in action before the complete destruction of the enemy on Iwo Jima. John "Doc" Bradley, was misidentified by his son James Bradley (with Ron Powers) as the sixth flag-raiser in his 2000 best seller, *Flags of Our Fathers*. The Department of Defense later identified the sixth flag-raiser as PFC Harold Schultz, but acknowledged Doc Bradley was indeed one of few actually present that historic day. Sadly, after several days atop the very windy Mt. Suribachi, the shredded flag was casually taken down and replaced with a new one. What became of the original flag remains unknown. Doc Bradley was awarded the Navy Cross for his "extraordinary heroism in action against the enemy" on Iwo Jima during close quarters combat on February 21, 1945 and was subsequently medically discharged from the Navy later that year.

AFTERWORD

It is widely held that the human spirit is the incorporeal or ethereal part of man. It includes our intellect, emotions, fears, passions, and creativity. Of all other living things, it provides us and only us, the ability to imagine and reflect. According to Genesis 2:7, the source of this remarkable power is the *breath of God*. It makes each of us an example of what is possible, while granting us the ability to inspire greatness in others. Therefore, our greatest contribution to those around us is in large part, our own excellence.

I thank them. I also thank you, the reader, for taking the time to read this book. If you liked it, I am hopeful you will share it with others. In that spirit of sharing, I, together with my publisher, AuthorVista LLC proudly donate a portion of the revenue from every book sold to these worthy organizations and others:

You can assist in this effort by sharing with me your inspiring quotes, quips, and virtue related stories. If new and appropriate material is provided I will happily use it in the future where possible, and of course attribute it accordingly.

> *When I stand before God at the end of my life,*
> *I would hope that I would not have a single*
> *bit of talent left, and I could say,*
> *'I used everything you gave me.'*
> *—Erma Bombeck*

SPECIAL OFFERS

CONTENT LICENSING OPPORTUNITIES

Good stories and quotes are powerful communication tools. A well-written, creative story or quote is capable of promoting a product, idea, service, organization or oneself. Inexpensive, non-expiring licenses enabling a licensee the use of material contained in this book are readily available and easy to obtain. For more information about licensing content, please contact the publisher via email at info@AuthorVista.com today.

BULK SALES

Whether you or your organization need a corporate gift, a unique fundraising tool, and/or unique promotional vehicle, you might find the hard work has already been done. AuthorVista, Inc. provides the opportunity to bypass the distributor or middlemen and sell bulk copy of this book and others directly to you or your organization. To learn more and find out how, email info@AuthorVista.com and put the words, Bulk Sales in the subject line.

.

ABOUT THE AUTHOR

Dr. Jonathan D. Rose received his B.S. in Engineering, B.A. in Chemistry, and M.S. in Electrical Engineering from the University of Detroit. He additionally received an M.F.S. (Master of Forensic Science) from National University, a Ph.D. in Biochemistry & Molecular Biology from the Medical College of Ohio, and his M.D. from Rush Medical University in Chicago, with a focus on forensic pathology. He is currently a licensed physician in two states.

Dr. Rose is a member of the National Internal Affairs Investigators Association, the International Association of Chiefs of Police, the International Homicide Investigators Association, the International Association of Hostage Negotiators, the International Association of Bloodstain Pattern Analysts, the International Law Enforcement Educators and Trainers Association, the International Crime Scene Investigators Association, the International Association for Identification, and the International Association of Arson Investigators. Dr. Rose is a practicing licensed private investigator in his home state of Michigan and is also a licensed investigator in California. He is a member of ASIS International and the Association of Certified Fraud Examiners. Dr. Rose is a distinguished security professional and holds all three of the ASIS International certifications (CPP, PSP, PCI). He is also a practicing Certified Fraud Examiner and security consultant.

Dr. Rose currently resides in Michigan but spends whatever time he can spare at his second home in the much warmer Southwest.

Made in the USA
Middletown, DE
01 March 2023

25569563R00097